The Virtues

The Virtues

POPE BENEDICT XVI

COLLECTED AND EDITED BY JACQUELYN LINDSEY

Our Sunday Visitor Publishing Division
Our Sunday Visitor, Inc.
Huntington, Indiana 46750

Copyright © 2010 by Our Sunday Visitor Publishing Division
Our Sunday Visitor, Inc. Published 2010

15 14 13 12 11 10   1 2 3 4 5 6 7 8 9

ISBN 978-1-59276-794-6 (Inventory No. T1099)
LCCN: 2010936165

Cover design by Lindsey Riesen
Interior design by M. Urgo

Cover art: *Detail of Prudence*
from the Lunette in the Sala dell'Udienza, 1496–1500 (fresco)
by Pietro Perugino (c. 1445–1523)
Collegio del Cambio, Perugia, Italy / Alinari / The Bridgeman Art Library
Nationality / copyright status: Italian / out of copyright

PRINTED IN THE UNITED STATES OF AMERICA

CONTENTS

Abbreviations

General Abbreviations

CCC — *Catechism of the Catholic Church*
DV — *Dei Verbum*, Dogmatic Constitution on Divine Revelation, Vatican II document
Deus Caritas Est — "God Is Love," Encyclical, December 25, 2005
Spe Salvi — "Saved in Hope," Encyclical, November 30, 2007

Scripture Abbreviations

Old Testament

Dt — Deuteronomy
Ez — Ezra
Hos — Hosea
Lev — Leviticus
Prov — Proverbs
Ps — Psalms
Sir — Sirach (Ecclesiasticus)
Wis — Wisdom
Zech — Zechariah

New Testament

Col — Colossians
Cor — Corinthians
Eph — Ephesians

Gal — Galatians
Jn — John
Lk — Luke
Mt — Matthew
Pet — Peter
Phil — Philippians
Rev — Revelation
Rom — Romans
Thess — Thessalonians
Tim — Timothy
Tit — Titus

INTRODUCTION

Virtue is a habitual and firm
disposition to do good.
(*CCC* 1833)

■

So faith, hope, love abide, these three;
but the greatest of these is love.
(*1 Cor* 13:13)

Pope Benedict XVI has regularly woven the theme of the virtues throughout his writings and speeches. This book highlights just some of the jewels of the Holy Father's teachings on the Theological Virtues of Faith, Hope, and Charity and the Cardinal Virtues of Prudence, Justice, Fortitude, and Temperance.

The world would do well to focus more intently on the Theological and Cardinal Virtues. As the *Catechism of the Catholic Church* reminds us: "A virtue is an habitual and firm disposition to do the good. It allows the person not only to perform good acts, but to give the best of himself. The virtuous person tends toward the good with all his sensory and spiritual powers; he pursues the good and chooses it in concrete actions. 'The goal of a virtuous life is to become like God' (St. Gregory of Nyssa, *De beatitudinibus*, 1:PG 44, 1200D)" (*CCC* 1803).

Leading a virtuous life leads to God. The Holy Father offers us the roadmap to get there through the Virtues.

Those of us still on our earthly pilgrimage are not called to mediocrity. We were created for greatness, for the sublime, to eventually be with Our Lord throughout eternity.

In his letter to the Philippians, St. Paul reminds us: "Whatever is true, whatever is honorable, whatever is just, whatever is pure, whatever is lovely, whatever is gracious, if there is any excellence, if there is anything worthy of praise, think about these things" (4:8). May this book be a vehicle to do just that through the words of the Holy Father, Pope Benedict XVI.

— Jacquelyn Lindsey, Editor

CREATED IN GOD'S IMAGE

Faith, hope, and charity go together. Hope is practiced through the virtue of patience, which continues to do good even in the face of apparent failure, and through the virtue of humility, which accepts God's mystery and trusts him even at times of darkness. Faith tells us that God has given his Son for our sakes and gives us the victorious certainty that it is really true: God is love! It thus transforms our impatience and our doubts into the sure hope that God holds the world in his hands and that, as the dramatic imagery of the end of the Book of Revelation points out, in spite of all darkness he ultimately triumphs in glory. Faith, which sees the love of God revealed in the pierced heart of Jesus on the Cross, gives rise to love. Love is the light — and in the end, the only light — that can always illuminate a world grown dim and give us the courage needed to keep living and working. Love is possible, and we are able to practice it because we are created in the image of God.

ENCYCLICAL, *DEUS CARITAS EST,* NO. 39

PART ONE

THE THEOLOGICAL VIRTUES

Faith, Hope, and Charity (Love)

There are three theological virtues: faith,
hope, and charity. They inform all the
moral virtues and give life to them.
(*CCC* 1841)

■

But, since we belong to the day, let us be
sober, and put on the breastplate of faith
and love, and for a helmet the hope of
salvation. (*1 Thess* 5:8)

Faith
Faith is the theological virtue by which we believe in God
and believe all that he has said and revealed to us, and that
Holy Church proposes for our belief, because he is truth
itself. By faith "man freely commits his entire self to God"
(*DV* 5).

CCC 1814

Hope
Hope is the theological virtue by which we desire the kingdom of heaven and eternal life as our happiness, placing
our trust in Christ's promises and relying not on our own
strength, but on the help of the grace of the Holy Spirit.
"Let us hold fast the confession of our hope without

wavering, for he who promised is faithful" (*Heb* 10:23).
"The Holy Spirit ... he poured out upon us richly through
Jesus Christ our Savior, so that we might be justified by his
grace and become heirs in hope of eternal life" (*Titus* 3:6–7).

CCC 1817

Charity
Charity is the theological virtue by which we love God
above all things for his own sake, and our neighbor as ourselves for the love of God.

CCC 1822

Keep Faith, Love, and Hope Alive

The Holy Spirit, who is eternal charity, the bond of unity
in the Trinity, with his power of divine charity unites scat-
tered humanity thereby creating the vast multiform community of the Church throughout the world. In the days
following the Ascension of the Lord until Pentecost Sunday, the disciples, with Mary, were gathered in the Upper
Room to pray. They knew that they themselves could not
create or organize the Church: the Church had to be born
and organized by divine initiative; she is not created by
us, she is a gift of God. And this is likewise the only way
in which she creates unity, a unity that must grow. The
Church in every time — and particularly in these nine
days between the Ascension and Pentecost — is spiritually
united in the Upper Room with the Apostles and Mary

to ceaselessly implore the outpouring of the Holy Spirit. Driven onwards by his mighty wind she will thus be able to proclaim the Gospel to the very ends of the earth.

This is why even in the face of difficulties and divisions, Christians cannot be resigned nor yield to discouragement. The Lord asks this of us: to persevere in prayer in order to keep alive the flame of faith, love, and hope which nourishes the desire for full unity. *"Ut unum sint!"* (That all may be one), says the Lord. May Christ's invitation always resound in our hearts, an invitation I was able to relaunch on my recent Apostolic Journey in the United States of America, when I referred to the centrality of prayer in the ecumenical movement. In this epoch of globalization and at the same time of fragmentation, "without [prayer], ecumenical structures, institutions, and programs would be deprived of their heart and soul" (*Ecumenical Prayer Service and Meeting*, St. Joseph's Church, New York, April 18, 2008). Let us give thanks to the Lord for the goals reached in ecumenical dialogue thanks to the Holy Spirit's action; let us be docile, listening to his voice so that our hearts, filled with hope, may continuously seek the path that leads to the full communion of all Christ's disciples.

In his Letter to the Galatians, St. Paul recalls that "the fruit of the Spirit is love, joy, peace, patience, kindness, goodness, faithfulness, gentleness, self-control" (*Gal* 5:22–23). These are the gifts of the Holy Spirit that we also implore today for all Christians, so that in the common and generous service to the Gospel, they may be a sign of God's love for humanity in the world. Let us turn our gaze confidently to

Mary, the Shrine of the Holy Spirit, and through her pray:
"Come, Holy Spirit, fill the hearts of your faithful and kin-
dle in them the fire of your love." Amen.

AUDIENCE, MAY 7, 2008

VIRTUES IN CHILDREN

Dear parents, I thank the Lord with you for the gift of these
children, and I invoke his assistance so that he may help
you to raise them and incorporate them into the spiritual
Body of the Church. As you offer them what they need
for their growth and salvation, may you always be committed, helped by their godparents, to developing in them
faith, hope, and charity, the theological virtues proper to
the new life given to them in the Sacrament of Baptism.

HOMILY, JANUARY 13, 2008

TRINITY OF VIRTUES

The last step of the ladder (30) [Step 30 of *The Ladder of
Divine Ascent* by St. John Climacus], suffused with "the
sober inebriation of the spirit," is dedicated to the supreme
"trinity of virtues": faith, hope, and above all charity. John
also speaks of charity as *eros* (human love), a symbol of
the matrimonial union of the soul with God, and once
again chooses the image of fire to express the fervor, light,
and purification of love for God. The power of human
love can be reoriented to God, just as a cultivated olive

may be grafted on to a wild olive tree (cf. *Rom* 11:24) (cf. 15, 66; 893). John is convinced that an intense experience of this *eros* will help the soul to advance far more than the harsh struggle against the passions because of its great power. Thus, in our journey, the positive aspect prevails. Yet charity is also seen in close relation to hope: "Hope is the power that drives love. Thanks to hope, we can look forward to the reward of charity.... Hope is the doorway of love.... The absence of hope destroys charity: our efforts are bound to it, our labors are sustained by it, and through it we are enveloped by the mercy of God" (30, 16; 1157). The conclusion of the *Ladder* contains the synthesis of the work in words that the author has God himself utter: "May this ladder teach you the spiritual disposition of the virtues. I am at the summit of the ladder, and as my great initiate (St. Paul) said: *"So faith, hope, love abide, these three; but the greatest of these is love"* (*1 Cor 13:13)!"* (30, 18; 1160).

At this point, a last question must be asked: can the *Ladder,* a work written by a hermit monk who lived 1,400 years ago, say something to us today? Can the existential journey of a man who lived his entire life on Mount Sinai in such a distant time be relevant to us? At first glance it would seem that the answer must be "no," because John Climacus is too remote from us. But if we look a little closer, we see that the monastic life is only a great symbol of baptismal life, of Christian life. It shows, so to speak, in capital letters what we write day after day in small letters. It is a prophetic symbol that reveals what the life of the baptized person is, in communion with Christ, with his death and Resurrection. The fact that the top of the "ladder," the final steps, are at the same time the fundamental, initial, and most simple virtues is particularly important to me: faith, hope, and charity. These are not virtues accessible only to moral heroes; rather they are gifts of God to all the baptized: in them our life develops too. The beginning is also the end, the starting point is also the point of arrival: the whole journey towards an ever more radical realization of faith, hope, and charity. The whole ascent is present in these virtues. Faith is fundamental, because this virtue implies that I renounce my arrogance, my thought, and the claim to judge by myself without entrusting myself to others. This journey towards humility, towards spiritual childhood is essential. It is necessary to overcome the attitude of arrogance that makes one say: I know better, in this my time of the 21st century, than what people could have known then. Instead, it is necessary to entrust oneself to Sacred Scripture alone, to the word of the Lord, to look out on the horizon of faith with humility, in order to enter into the enormous immensity of the universal world, of the world of God. In this way our soul grows, the sensitivity of the heart grows toward God. Rightly, John Climacus says that hope alone renders us capable of living charity; hope in which we transcend the things of every day, we do not expect success in our earthly days but we look forward to the revelation of God himself at last. It is only in this extension of our soul, in this self-transcendence, that our life becomes great and that we are able to bear the effort and disappointments of every day, that we can be kind to others without expecting any reward. Only if there is God, this great hope to which I aspire, can I take the small steps of my life and thus learn charity. The mystery of prayer, of the personal knowledge of Jesus, is concealed in charity: simple prayer that strives only to move the divine Teacher's heart. So it is that one's own heart opens, one learns from him his own kindness, his love. Let us therefore use this "ascent" of faith, hope, and charity. In this way we will arrive at true life.

GENERAL AUDIENCE, FEBRUARY 11, 2009

DIALOGUE WITH OTHER FAITHS

The Church shares these observations with other religions. Motivated by charity, she approaches dialogue believing that the true source of freedom is found in the person of Jesus of Nazareth. Christians believe it is he who fully discloses the human potential for virtue and goodness, and he who liberates us from sin and darkness. The universality of human experience, which transcends all geographical boundaries and cultural limitations, makes it possible for followers of religions to engage in dialogue so as to grapple with the mystery of life's joys and sufferings. In this regard, the Church eagerly seeks opportunities to listen to the spiritual experience of other religions. We could say that all religions aim to penetrate the profound meaning of human existence by linking it to an origin or principle outside itself. Religions offer an attempt to understand the cosmos as coming from and returning to this origin or principle. Christians believe that God has revealed this origin and principle in Jesus, whom the Bible refers to as the "Alpha and Omega" (cf. *Rev* 1:8; 22:1).

ADDRESS, JULY 18, 2008

CHAPTER 1

FAITH

By faith, we believe in God and believe
all that he has revealed to us and that
Holy Church proposes for our belief.
(*CCC* 1842)

∎

For I am not ashamed of the gospel:
it is the power of God for salvation to
every one who has faith, to the Jew first
and also to the Greek. For in it the
righteousness of God is revealed through
faith for faith; as it is written,
"He who through faith is righteous
shall live." (*Rom* 1:16–17)

BEING GUIDED BY THE SPIRIT

Only sincere dialogue, open to the truth of the Gospel, could guide the Church on her journey: "For the kingdom of God does not mean food and drink but righteousness and peace and joy in the Holy Spirit" (*Rom* 14:17). It is a lesson that we too must learn: with the different charisms

entrusted to Peter and to Paul, let us all allow ourselves to
be guided by the Spirit, seeking to live in the freedom that
is guided by faith in Christ and expressed in service to the
brethren. It is essential to be conformed ever more closely
to Christ. In this way one becomes really free, in this way
the Law's deepest core is expressed within us: love for God
and neighbor. Let us pray the Lord that he will teach us to
share his sentiments, to learn from him true freedom and
the evangelical love that embraces every human being.

GENERAL AUDIENCE, OCTOBER 1, 2008

HEROIC FAITH

When Christians are truly the leaven, light, and salt of the
earth, they too become the object of persecution, as was
Jesus; like him they are "a sign of contradiction." Fraternal
life in common and the love, faith, and decisions in favor
of the lowliest and poorest that mark the existence of the
Christian community sometimes give rise to violent aversion. How useful it is then to look to the shining witness
of those who have preceded us in the sign of heroic fidelity
to the point of martyrdom!

HOMILY, APRIL 7, 2008

A VARIETY OF VOCATIONS

Throughout the centuries many men and women, transformed by divine love, have consecrated their lives to the

cause of the Kingdom. Already on the shores of the Sea of Galilee, many allowed themselves to be won by Jesus: they were in search of healing in body or spirit, and they were touched by the power of his grace. Others were chosen personally by Him and became his apostles. We also find some, like Mary Magdalene and others, who followed him on their own initiative, simply out of love. Like the disciple John, they too found a special place in his heart. These men and women, who knew the mystery of the love of the Father through Jesus, represent the variety of vocations which have always been present in the Church. The model of one called to give witness in a particular manner to the love of God, is Mary, the Mother of Jesus, who in her pilgrimage of faith is directly associated with the mystery of the Incarnation and Redemption.

HOMILY, MAY 7, 2006

COOPERATING IN EVANGELIZATION

The gift of faith calls all Christians to cooperate in the work of evangelization. This awareness must be nourished by preaching and catechesis, by the liturgy, and by constant formation in prayer. It must grow through the practice of welcoming others, with charity and spiritual companionship, through reflection and discernment, as well as pastoral planning, of which attention to vocations must be an integral part.

MESSAGE, APRIL 13, 2008

JUSTICE IN POLITICS

Justice is both the aim and the intrinsic criterion of all politics. Politics is more than a mere mechanism for defining the rules of public life: its origin and its goal are found in justice, which by its very nature has to do with ethics. The State must inevitably face the question of how justice can be achieved here and now. But this presupposes an even more radical question: what is justice? The problem is one of practical reason; but if reason is to be exercised properly, it must undergo constant purification, since it can never be completely free of the danger of a certain ethical blindness caused by the dazzling effect of power and special interests.

Here politics and faith meet. Faith by its specific nature is an encounter with the living God — an encounter opening up new horizons extending beyond the sphere of reason. But it is also a purifying force for reason itself. From God's standpoint, faith liberates reason from its blind spots and therefore helps it to be ever more fully itself. Faith enables reason to do its work more effectively and to see its proper object more clearly. This is where Catholic social doctrine has its place: it has no intention of giving the Church power over the State. Even less is it an attempt to impose on those who do not share the faith ways of thinking and modes of conduct proper to faith. Its aim is simply to help purify reason and to contribute, here and now, to the acknowledgment and attainment of what is just.

ENCYCLICAL, *DEUS CARITAS EST,* No. 28

Mary's Faith

Let us ask Mary today to make us the gift of her faith, that faith which enables us already to live in the dimension between finite and infinite, that faith which also transforms the sentiment of time and the passing of our existence, that faith in which we are profoundly aware that our life is not retracted by the past but attracted towards the future, towards God, where Christ, and behind him Mary, has preceded us.

HOMILY, AUGUST 15, 2008

The Present and the Future

Faith is not merely a personal reaching out towards things to come that are still totally absent: it gives us something. It gives us even now something of the reality we are waiting for, and this present reality constitutes for us a "proof" of the things that are still unseen. Faith draws the future into the present, so that it is no longer simply a "not yet." The fact that this future exists changes the present; the present is touched by the future reality, and thus the things of the future spill over into those of the present and those of the present into those of the future.

ENCYCLICAL, *SPE SALVI*, No. 7

Living by Faith in the Son of God

It is not science that redeems man: man is redeemed by love. This applies even in terms of this present world.

When someone has the experience of a great love in his life, this is a moment of "redemption" which gives a new meaning to his life. But soon he will also realize that the love bestowed upon him cannot by itself resolve the question of his life. It is a love that remains fragile. It can be destroyed by death. The human being needs unconditional love. He needs the certainty which makes him say: "neither death, nor life, nor angels, nor principalities, nor things present, nor things to come, nor powers, nor height, nor depth, nor anything else in all creation, will be able to separate us from the love of God in Christ Jesus our Lord" (*Rom* 8:38–39). If this absolute love exists, with its absolute certainty, then — only then — is man "redeemed," whatever should happen to him in his particular circumstances. This is what it means to say: Jesus Christ has "redeemed" us. Through him we have become certain of God, a God who is not a remote "first cause" of the world, because his only-begotten Son has become man and of him everyone can say: "I live by faith in the Son of God, who loved me and gave himself for me" (*Gal* 2:20).

ENCYCLICAL, *SPE SALVI*, NO. 26

PEOPLE OF SOUND FAITH NEEDED

The Church thus urgently needs people with a deep and sound faith, a well-grounded culture and genuine human and social sensitivity, of Religious and priests who dedicate their lives to being on these very frontiers to bear witness and to help people understand that on the contrary there is profound harmony between faith and reason, between the Gospel spirit, the thirst for justice and initiatives for peace. Only in this way will it be possible to make the Lord's true Face known to the many for whom he is still concealed or unrecognizable.

ADDRESS, FEBRUARY 21, 2008

IN TRUTH AND SIMPLICITY

The Virgin Mary's maternal love disarms all pride; it renders man capable of seeing himself as he is, and it inspires in him the desire to be converted so as to give glory to God.

Thus, Mary shows us the right way to come to the Lord. She teaches us to approach him in truth and simplicity. Thanks to her, we discover that the Christian faith is not a burden: it is like a wing which enables us to fly higher, so as to take refuge in God's embrace.

ANGELUS, SEPTEMBER 14, 2008

PRAYER FOR VOCATIONS

O Father, raise up among Christians
abundant and holy vocations to the priesthood,
who keep the faith alive
and guard the blessed memory of your Son Jesus

through the preaching of his word
and the administration of the Sacraments,
with which you continually renew your faithful.

Grant us holy ministers of your altar,
who are careful and fervent guardians of the Eucharist,
the sacrament of the supreme gift of Christ
for the redemption of the world.

Call ministers of your mercy,
who, through the sacrament of Reconciliation,
spread the joy of your forgiveness.

Grant, O Father, that the Church may welcome with joy
the numerous inspirations of the Spirit of your Son
and, docile to His teachings,
may she care for vocations to the ministerial priesthood
and to the consecrated life.

Sustain the Bishops, priests, and deacons,
consecrated men and women, and all the baptized in Christ,
so that they may faithfully fulfill their mission
at the service of the Gospel.

This we pray through Christ our Lord. Amen.

Mary, Queen of Apostles, pray for us.

MESSAGE FOR THE FORTY-THIRD WORLD DAY
OF PRAYER FOR VOCATIONS, MAY 7, 2006

Falling in Love with Christ

From the Basilica of Saint Francis in which his mortal remains repose, I would now like above all to make his tones of praise my own: "Most High, All Powerful, All Good Lord, All praise is yours, all glory, all honor, and all blessing" (cf. *Canticle of the Sun* 1). Francis of Assisi is a great teacher of our faith and praise. By falling in love with Jesus Christ he encountered the Face of God-Love, of whom he became an impassioned bard and sang his praise passionately like a real "minstrel of God."

In the light of the Gospel Beatitudes we can understand the gentleness with which St. Francis was able to live his relations with others, presenting himself in humility to all and becoming a witness and artisan of peace.

ANGELUS, JUNE 17, 2007

Be Docile to the Power of the Spirit

May each one of you rediscover God as the sense and foundation of every creature, light of truth, flame of charity, bond of unity, like the hymn of the *Agorà* of the Italian youth. May you be docile to the power of the Spirit! He, the Holy Spirit, the Protagonist of the World Youth Day at Sydney; he makes you witnesses of Christ. Not in word but in deed, with a new type of life. You will not be afraid any longer to lose your freedom, because you will live it fully by giving it away in love. You will no longer be attached to material goods, because you will feel within you the joy of sharing them. You will cease to be sad with the sadness of the world, but you will feel sorrow at evil and rejoice at goodness, especially for mercy and forgiveness. And if this happens, if you will have truly discovered God in the Face of Christ, you will no longer think of the Church as an institution external to you, but as your spiritual family, as we are living now, at this moment. This is the faith that your forefathers have handed down to you. This is the faith you are called to live today, in very different times.

ADDRESS, SEPTEMBER 7, 2008

LEARNING FROM MARY

This mystery — the Incarnation of the Word and the divine Motherhood of Mary — is great and certainly far from easy to understand with the human mind alone.

Yet, by learning from Mary, we can understand with our hearts what our eyes and minds do not manage to perceive or contain on their own. Indeed, this is such a great gift that only through faith are we granted to accept it, while not entirely understanding it. And it is precisely on this journey of faith that Mary comes to meet us as our support and guide. She is mother because she brought forth Jesus in the flesh; she is mother because she adhered totally to the Father's will. St. Augustine wrote: "The divine motherhood would have been of no value to her had Christ not borne her in his heart, with a destiny more fortunate than the moment when she conceived him in the flesh" (*De Sancta Virginitate*, 3, 3). And in her heart Mary continued to treasure, to "piece together" the subsequent events of which she was to be a witness and protagonist, even to the death on the Cross and the Resurrection of her Son Jesus.

HOMILY, JANUARY 1, 2008

CULTURE CHALLENGES THE GOSPEL

A serious commitment to evangelization cannot prescind from a profound diagnosis of the real challenges the Gospel encounters in contemporary American culture.

Of course, what is essential is a correct understanding of the just autonomy of the secular order, an autonomy which cannot be divorced from God the Creator and his saving plan (cf. *Gaudium et Spes*, 36). Perhaps America's brand of secularism poses a particular problem: it allows for professing belief in God, and respects the public role of religion and the Churches, but at the same time it can subtly reduce religious belief to a lowest common denominator. Faith becomes a passive acceptance that certain things "out there" are true, but without practical relevance for everyday life. The result is a growing separation of faith from life: living "as if God did not exist." This is aggravated by an individualistic and eclectic approach to faith and religion: far from a Catholic approach to "thinking with the Church," each person believes he or she has a right to pick and choose, maintaining external social bonds but without an integral, interior conversion to the law of Christ. Consequently, rather than being transformed and renewed in mind, Christians are easily tempted to conform themselves to the spirit of this age (cf. *Rom* 12:3). We have seen this emerge in an acute way in the scandal given by Catholics who promote an alleged right to abortion.

On a deeper level, secularism challenges the Church to reaffirm and to pursue more actively her mission in and to the world. As the Council made clear, the lay faithful have a particular responsibility in this regard. What is needed, I am convinced, is a greater sense of the intrinsic relationship between the Gospel and the natural law on the one hand, and, on the other, the pursuit of authentic human good, as embodied in civil law and in personal moral decisions. In a society that rightly values personal liberty, the Church needs to promote at every level of her teaching — in catechesis, preaching, seminary, and university instruction — an apologetics aimed at affirming the truth of Christian revelation, the harmony of faith and reason, and a sound understanding of freedom, seen in positive terms as a liberation both *from* the limitations of sin and *for* an authentic and fulfilling life. In a word, the Gospel has to be preached and taught as an integral way of life, offering an attractive and true answer, intellectually and practically, to real human problems. The "dictatorship of relativism," in the end, is nothing less than a threat to genuine human freedom, which only matures in generosity and fidelity to the truth.

Much more, of course, could be said on this subject: let me conclude, though, by saying that I believe that the Church in America, at this point in her history, is faced with the challenge of recapturing the Catholic vision of reality and presenting it, in an engaging and imaginative way, to a society which markets any number of recipes for human fulfillment. I think in particular of our need to speak to the hearts of young people, who, despite their constant exposure to messages contrary to the Gospel, continue to thirst for authenticity, goodness, and truth. Much remains to be done, particularly on the level of preaching and catechesis in parishes and schools, if the new evangelization is to bear fruit for the renewal of ecclesial life in America.

MEETING WITH U.S. BISHOPS, APRIL 16, 2008

MEDITATING DAY AND NIGHT

Personally, Cassiodorus dedicated himself to philosophical, theological, and exegetical studies without any special creativity, but was attentive to the insights he considered valid in others. He read Jerome and Augustine in particular with respect and devotion. Of the latter he said: "In Augustine there is such a great wealth of writings that it seems to me impossible to find anything that has not already been abundantly treated by him" (cf. *PL* 70, col. 10). Citing Jerome, on the other hand, he urged the monks of *Vivarium*: "It is not only those who fight to the point of bloodshed or who live in virginity who win the palm of victory but also all who, with God's help, triumph over physical vices and preserve their upright faith. But in order that you may always, with God's help, more easily overcome the world's pressures and enticements while remaining in it as pilgrims constantly journeying forward, seek first to guarantee for yourselves the salutary help suggested by the first Psalm which recommends meditation night and day on the law of the Lord. Indeed, the enemy will not find any gap through which to assault you if all your attention is taken up by Christ" (*De Institutione Divinarum Scripturarum,* 32: *PL* 70, col. 1147). This is a recommendation we can also accept as valid. In fact, we live in a time of intercultural encounter, of the danger of violence that destroys cultures, and of the necessary commitment to pass on important values and to teach the new generations the path of reconciliation and peace. We find this path by turning to the God with the human Face, the God who revealed himself to us in Christ.

GENERAL AUDIENCE, MARCH 12, 2008

THE FULFILLMENT OF CREATION

First, as you know, it is becoming more and more difficult, in our Western societies, to speak in a meaningful way of "salvation." Yet salvation — deliverance from the reality of evil and the gift of new life and freedom in Christ — is at the heart of the Gospel. We need to discover, as I have suggested, new and engaging ways of proclaiming this message and awakening a thirst for the fulfillment which only Christ can bring. It is in the Church's liturgy, and above all in the sacrament of the Eucharist, that these realities are most powerfully expressed and lived in the life of believers; perhaps we still have much to do in realizing the Council's vision of the liturgy as the exercise of the common priesthood and the impetus for a fruitful apostolate in the world.

Second, we need to acknowledge with concern the almost complete eclipse of an eschatological sense in many of our traditionally Christian societies. As you know, I have pointed to this problem in the Encyclical *Spe Salvi*. Suffice it to say that faith and hope are not limited to this world: as theological virtues, they unite us with the Lord and draw us toward the fulfillment not only of our personal destiny but also that of all creation. Faith and hope are the inspiration and basis of our efforts to prepare for the coming of the Kingdom of God. In Christianity, there can be no room for purely private religion: Christ is the Savior of the world, and, as members of his Body and sharers in his prophetic, priestly, and royal *munera*, we cannot separate our love for him from our commitment to the building up of the Church and the extension of his Kingdom. To the extent that religion becomes a purely private affair, it loses its very soul.

Let me conclude by stating the obvious. The fields are still ripe for harvesting (cf. *Jn* 4:35); God continues to give the growth (cf. *1 Cor* 3:6). We can and must believe, with the late Pope John Paul II, that God is preparing a new springtime for Christianity (cf. *Redemptoris Missio*, 86). What is needed above all, at this time in the history of the Church in America, is a renewal of that apostolic zeal which inspires her shepherds actively to seek out the lost, to bind up those who have been wounded, and to bring strength to those who are languishing (cf. *Ez* 34:16). And this, as I have said, calls for new ways of thinking based on a sound diagnosis of today's challenges and a commitment to unity in the service of the Church's mission to the present generation.

MEETING WITH THE BISHOPS OF THE U.S., APRIL 16, 2008

CHAPTER 2

HOPE

By hope we desire, and with steadfast trust await from God, eternal life and the graces to merit it. (*CCC* 1843)

∎

Rejoice in your hope, be patient in tribulation, be constant in prayer. (*Rom* 12:12)

IN CONTACT WITH GOD

In St. Thomas Aquinas' last work that remained unfinished, the *Compendium Theologiae* which he intended to structure simply according to the three theological virtues of faith, hope, and charity, the great Doctor began and partly developed his chapter on hope. In it he identified, so to speak, hope with prayer: the chapter on hope is at the same time the chapter on prayer.

Prayer is hope in action. And in fact, true reason is contained in prayer, which is why it is possible to hope: we can come into contact with the Lord of the world, he listens to us, and we can listen to him. This is what St.

Ignatius was alluding to and what I want to remind you of once again — the truly great thing in Christianity, which does not dispense one from small, daily things but must not be concealed by them either, is this ability to come into contact with God.

ADDRESS, NOVEMBER 9, 2006

HOPE THAT SUSTAINS LIFE

In this sense it is true that anyone who does not know God, even though he may entertain all kinds of hopes, is ultimately without hope, without the great hope that sustains the whole of life (cf. *Eph* 2:12). Man's great, true hope which holds firm in spite of all disappointments can only be God — God who has loved us and who continues to love us "to the end," until all "is accomplished" (cf. *Jn* 13:1 and 19:30). Whoever is moved by love begins to perceive what "life" really is. He begins to perceive the meaning of the word of hope that we encountered in the Baptismal Rite: from faith I await "eternal life" — the true life which, whole and unthreatened, in all its fullness, is simply life. Jesus, who said that he had come so that we might have life and have it in its fullness, in abundance (cf. *Jn* 10:10), has also explained to us what "life" means: "this is eternal life, that they know thee the only true God, and Jesus Christ whom you have sent" (*Jn* 17:3). Life in its true sense is not something we have exclusively in or from ourselves: it is a relationship. And life in its totality is a relationship with him who is the source of life. If we are in relation with him who does not die, who is Life itself and Love itself, then we are in life. Then we "live."

ENCYCLICAL, *SPE SALVI*, NO. 27

MARY: FIRST FRUIT OF HUMANITY

Mary is indeed the first fruit of the new humanity, the creature in whom the mystery of Christ — his Incarnation, death, Resurrection, and Ascension into Heaven — has already fully taken effect, redeeming her from death and conveying her, body and soul, to the Kingdom of immortal life. For this reason, as the Second Vatican Council recalls, the Virgin Mary is a sign of certain hope and comfort to us (cf. *Lumen Gentium*, no. 68). Today's feast impels us to lift our gaze to Heaven; not to a heaven consisting of abstract ideas or even an imaginary heaven created by art, but the Heaven of true reality which is God himself. God is Heaven. He is our destination, the destination and the eternal dwelling place from which we come and for which we are striving.

HOMILY, AUGUST 15, 2008

TRUSTWORTHY HOPE

"*SPE SALVI facti sumus*" — in hope we were saved, says Saint Paul to the Romans, and likewise to us (*Rom* 8:24). According to the Christian faith, "redemption" — salvation — is not simply a given. Redemption is offered to us in the sense that we have been given hope, trustworthy hope, by virtue of which we can face our present: the present, even if it is arduous, can be lived and accepted if it leads towards a goal, if we can be sure of this goal, and if this goal is great enough to justify the effort of the journey.

ENCYCLICAL, SPE SALVI, No. 1

GOD IS THE GREAT HOPE

Let us say once again: we need the greater and lesser hopes that keep us going day by day. But these are not enough without the great hope, which must surpass everything else. This great hope can only be God, who encompasses the whole of reality and who can bestow upon us what we, by ourselves, cannot attain. The fact that it comes to us as a gift is actually part of hope. God is the foundation of hope: not any god, but the God who has a human face and who has loved us to the end, each one of us and humanity in its entirety. His Kingdom is not an imaginary hereafter, situated in a future that will never arrive; his Kingdom is present wherever he is loved and wherever his love reaches us. His love alone gives us the possibility of soberly persevering day by day, without ceasing to be spurred on by hope, in a world which by its very nature is imperfect. His love is at the same time our guarantee of the existence of what we only vaguely sense and which nevertheless, in our deepest self, we await: a life that is "truly" life.

ENCYCLICAL, SPE SALVI, No. 31

LOVE AND LIFE

Yes, true hope is only born from the Blood of Christ and blood poured out for him. There is blood which is the sign of death, but there is also blood that expresses love and life. The Blood of Jesus and the blood of the Martyrs, like that of your own beloved Patron St. Januarius, is a source of new life. I would like to conclude by making my own a saying from your Archbishop's Pastoral Letter that sounds like this: "The seed of hope may be the tiniest but can give life to a flourishing tree and bear abundant fruit." This seed exists and is active in Naples, despite the problems and difficulties. Let us pray to the Lord that he will cause an authentic faith and firm hope to grow in the Christian community that can effectively oppose discouragement and violence. Naples certainly needs appropriate political interventions, but first it needs a profound spiritual renewal; it needs believers who put their full trust back in God and with his help work hard to spread Gospel values in society. Let us ask Mary's help with this, as well as that of your holy Protectors, especially St. Januarius. Amen!

HOMILY, OCTOBER 21, 2007

STAR OF HOPE

Human life is a journey. Towards what destination? How do we find the way? Life is like a voyage on the sea of history, often dark and stormy, a voyage in which we watch for the stars that indicate the route. The true stars of our life are the people who have lived good lives. They are lights of hope. Certainly, Jesus Christ is the true light, the sun that has risen above all the shadows of history. But to reach him we also need lights close by — people who shine with his light and so guide us along our way. Who more than Mary could be a star of hope for us? With her "yes" she opened the door of our world to God himself; she became the living Ark of the Covenant, in whom God took flesh, became one of us, and pitched his tent among us (cf. *Jn* 1:14).

ENCYCLICAL, SPE SALVI, NO. 49

PURIFICATION OF PURGATORY

The souls of the departed can, however, receive "solace and refreshment" through the Eucharist, prayer, and almsgiving. The belief that love can reach into the afterlife, that reciprocal giving and receiving is possible, in which our affection for one another continues beyond the limits of death — this has been a fundamental conviction of Christianity throughout the ages, and it remains a source of comfort today. Who would not feel the need to convey to their departed loved ones a sign of kindness, a gesture of gratitude or even a request for pardon? Now a further question arises: if "Purgatory" is simply purification through fire in the encounter with the Lord, Judge and Savior, how can a third person intervene, even if he or she is particularly close to the other? When we ask such a question, we should recall that no man is an island, entire of itself. Our lives are involved with one another, through innumerable interactions they are linked together. No one lives alone. No one sins alone. No one is saved alone. The lives of others continually spill over into mine: in what I think, say, do, and achieve. And conversely, my life spills over into that of others: for better and for worse. So my prayer for another is not something extraneous to that person, something external, not even after death. In the interconnectedness of Being, my gratitude to the other — my prayer for him — can play a small part in his purification. And for that there is no need to convert earthly time into God's time: in the communion of souls simple terrestrial time is superseded. It is never too late to touch the heart of another, nor is it ever in vain. In this way we further clarify an important element of the Christian concept of hope. Our hope is always essentially also hope for others; only thus is it truly hope for me too (cf. *CCC* 1032). As Christians we should never limit ourselves to asking: how can I save myself? We should also ask: what can I do in order that others may be saved and that for them too the star of hope may rise? Then I will have done my utmost for my own personal salvation as well.

ENCYCLICAL, *SPE SALVI,* NO. 48

TRUE FRIENDSHIP

The so-called prosperity of the wicked is therefore proven to be false (Bk IV), and the providential nature of *adversa fortuna* is highlighted. Life's difficulties not only reveal how transient and short-lived life is, but are even shown to serve for identifying and preserving authentic relations among human beings. *Adversa fortuna,* in fact, makes it possible to discern false friends from true and makes one realize that nothing is more precious to the human being than a true friendship. The fatalistic acceptance of a condition of suffering is nothing short of perilous, the believer Boethius added, because "it eliminates at its roots the very possibility of prayer and of theological hope, which form the basis of man's relationship with God" (Bk V, 3: *PL* 63, col. 842).

GENERAL AUDIENCE ON BOETHIUS AND CASSIODORUS,
MARCH 12, 2008

LEARN HOPE THROUGH PRAYER

A first essential setting for learning hope is prayer. When no one listens to me any more, God still listens to me. When I can no longer talk to anyone or call upon anyone, I can always talk to God. When there is no longer anyone to help me deal with a need or expectation that goes beyond the human capacity for hope, he can help me (cf. *CCC* 2657). When I have been plunged into complete solitude...; if I pray I am never totally alone.

ENCYCLICAL, *SPE SALVI,* NO. 32

AN EXERCISE OF DESIRE

Saint Augustine, in a homily on the *First Letter of John*, describes very beautifully the intimate relationship between prayer and hope. He defines prayer as an exercise of desire. Man was created for greatness — for God himself; he was created to be filled by God. But his heart is too small for the greatness to which it is destined. It must be stretched. "By delaying [his gift], God strengthens our desire; through desire he enlarges our soul, and by expanding it he increases its capacity [for receiving him]." Augustine refers to Saint Paul, who speaks of himself as straining forward to the things that are to come (cf. *Phil* 3:13). He then uses a very beautiful image to describe this process of enlargement and preparation of the human heart. "Suppose that God wishes to fill you with honey [a symbol of God's tenderness and goodness]; but if you are full of vinegar, where will you put the honey?" The vessel, that is your heart, must first be enlarged and then cleansed, freed from the vinegar and its taste. This requires hard work and is painful, but in this way alone do we become suited to that for which we are destined (cf. *In 1 Ioannis* 4, 6: *PL* 35, 2008f). Even if Augustine speaks directly only of our capacity for God, it is nevertheless clear that through this effort by which we are freed from vinegar and the taste of vinegar, not only are we made free for God, but we also become open to others. It is only by becoming children of God, that we can be with our common Father. To pray is not to step outside history and withdraw to our own private corner of happiness. When we pray properly we undergo a process of inner purification which opens us up to God and thus to our fellow human beings as well. In prayer we must learn what we can truly ask of God — what is worthy of God. We must learn that we cannot pray against others. We must learn that we cannot ask for the superficial and comfortable things that we desire at this moment — that meager, misplaced hope that leads us away from God. We must learn to purify our desires and our hopes. We must free ourselves from the hidden lies with which we deceive ourselves. God sees through them, and when we come before God, we too are forced to recognize them. "But who can discern his errors? Clear thou me from hidden faults" prays the Psalmist (*Ps* 19:12 [18:13]). Failure to recognize my guilt, the illusion of my innocence, does not justify me and does not save me, because I am culpable for the numbness of my conscience and my incapacity to recognize the evil in me for what it is. If God does not exist, perhaps I have to seek refuge in these lies, because there is no one who can forgive me; no one who is the true criterion. Yet my encounter with God awakens my conscience in such a way that it no longer aims at self-justification, and is no longer a mere reflection of me and those of my contemporaries who shape my thinking, but it becomes a capacity for listening to the Good itself.

ENCYCLICAL, *SPE SALVI*, No. 33

MARY'S GIFT OF LIGHT AND HOPE

Mary, in whose virginal womb God was made man, is our Mother! Indeed, from the Cross before bringing his sacrifice to completion, Jesus gave her to us as our Mother and entrusted us to her as her children. This is a mystery of mercy and love, a gift that enriches the Church with fruitful spiritual motherhood. Let us turn our gaze to her, especially today, dear brothers and sisters, and imploring her help, prepare ourselves to treasure all her maternal teaching. Does not our Heavenly Mother invite us to shun evil and to do good, following with docility the divine law engraved in every Christian's heart? Does not she, who preserved her hope even at the peak of her trial, ask us not to lose heart when suffering and death come knocking at the door of our homes? Does she not ask us to look confidently to our future? Does not the Immaculate Virgin exhort us to be brothers and sisters to one another, all united by the commitment to build together a world that is more just, supportive, and peaceful?

Yes, dear friends! On this solemn day, the Church once again holds up Mary to the world as a sign of sure hope and of the definitive victory of good over evil. The one whom we invoke as "full of grace" reminds us that we are all brothers and sisters and that God is our Creator and our Father. Without him, or even worse, against him, we human beings will never be able to find the way that leads to love, we will never be able to defeat the power of hatred and violence, we will never be able to build a lasting peace.

May the people of every nation and culture welcome this message of light and hope: may they accept it as a gift from the hands of Mary, Mother of all humanity. If life is a journey and this journey is often dark, difficult, and exhausting, what star can illuminate it? In my Encyclical *Spe Salvi*, published at the beginning of Advent, I wrote that the Church looks to Mary and calls on her as a "star of hope" (no. 49). During our common voyage on the sea of history, we stand in need of "lights of hope," that is, of people who shine with Christ's light and "so guide us along our way" (*ibid.*). And who could be a better "Star of Hope" for us than Mary? With her "yes," with the generous offering of freedom received from the Creator, she enabled the hope of the millennia to become reality, to enter this world and its history. Through her God took flesh, became one of us, and pitched his tent among us.

Thus, inspired by filial trust, we say to her: "Teach us, Mary, to believe, to hope, to love with you; show us the way that leads to peace, the way to the Kingdom of Jesus. You, Star of Hope, who wait for us anxiously in the everlasting light of the eternal Homeland, shine upon us and guide us through daily events, now and at the hour of our death. Amen!"

ADDRESS, DECEMBER 8, 2007

WITNESSES OF HOPE

Certainly, in our many different sufferings and trials we always need the lesser and greater hopes too — a kind visit, the healing of internal and external wounds, a favorable resolution of a crisis, and so on. In our lesser trials these kinds of hope may even be sufficient. But in truly great trials, where I must make a definitive decision to place the truth before my own welfare, career, and possessions, I need the certitude of that true, great hope of which we

have spoken here. For this too we need witnesses — martyrs — who have given themselves totally, so as to show
us the way — day after day. We need them if we are to
prefer goodness to comfort, even in the little choices we
face each day — knowing that this is how we live life to
the full. Let us say it once again: the capacity to suffer for
the sake of the truth is the measure of humanity. Yet this
capacity to suffer depends on the type and extent of the
hope that we bear within us and build upon. The saints
were able to make the great journey of human existence in
the way that Christ had done before them, because they
were brimming with great hope.

ENCYCLICAL, *SPE SALVI*. NO. 39

IN THE SERVICE OF PEACE

God is the unfailing source of the hope which gives meaning to personal and community life. God, and God alone,
brings to fulfillment every work of good and of peace. History has amply demonstrated that declaring war on God
in order to eradicate him from human hearts only leads
a fearful and impoverished humanity toward decisions
which are ultimately futile. This realization must impel
believers in Christ to become convincing witnesses of the
God who is inseparably truth and love, placing themselves
at the service of peace in broad cooperation with other
Christians, the followers of other religions and with all
men and women of good will.

WORLD DAY OF PEACE MESSAGE, JANUARY 1, 2006

The Kingdom of God Is a Gift

All serious and upright human conduct is hope in action. This is so first of all in the sense that we thereby strive to realize our lesser and greater hopes, to complete this or that task which is important for our onward journey, or we work towards a brighter and more humane world so as to open doors into the future. Yet our daily efforts in pursuing our own lives and in working for the world's future either tire us or turn into fanaticism, unless we are enlightened by the radiance of the great hope that cannot be destroyed even by small-scale failures or by a breakdown in matters of historic importance. If we cannot hope for more than is effectively attainable at any given time, or more than is promised by political or economic authorities, our lives will soon be without hope. It is important to know that I can always continue to hope, even if in my own life, or the historical period in which I am living, there seems to be nothing left to hope for. Only the great certitude of hope that my own life and history in general, despite all failures, are held firm by the indestructible power of Love, and that this gives them their meaning and importance, only this kind of hope can then give the courage to act and to persevere. Certainly we cannot "build" the Kingdom of God by our own efforts — what we build will always be the kingdom of man with all the limitations proper to our human nature. The Kingdom of God is a gift, and precisely because of this, it is great and beautiful, and constitutes the response to our hope. And we cannot — to use the classical expression — "merit" Heaven through our works. Heaven is always more than we could merit, just as being loved is never something "merited," but always a gift. However, even when we are fully aware that Heaven far exceeds what we can merit, it will always be true that our behavior is not indifferent before God and therefore is not indifferent for the unfolding of history. We can open ourselves and the world and allow God to enter: we can open ourselves to truth, to love, to what is good. This is what the saints did, those who, as "God's fellow workers," contributed to the world's salvation (cf. *1 Cor* 3:9; *1 Thess* 3:2). We can free our life and the world from the poisons and contaminations that could destroy the present and the future. We can uncover the sources of creation and keep them unsullied, and in this way we can make a right use of creation, which comes to us as a gift, according to its intrinsic requirements and ultimate purpose. This makes sense even if outwardly we achieve nothing or seem powerless in the face of overwhelming hostile forces. So on the one hand, our actions engender hope for us and for others; but at the same time, it is the great hope based upon God's promises that gives us courage and directs our action in good times and bad.

ENCYCLICAL, SPE SALVI, NO. 35

JUDGMENT AND GRACE

The judgment of God is hope, both because it is justice and because it is grace. If it were merely grace, making all earthly things cease to matter, God would still owe us an answer to the question about justice — the crucial question that we ask of history and of God. If it were merely justice, in the end it could bring only fear to us all. The incarnation of God in Christ has so closely linked the two together — judgment and grace — that justice is firmly established: we all work out our salvation "with fear and trembling" (*Phil* 2:12). Nevertheless grace allows us all to hope, and to go trustfully to meet the Judge whom we know as our "advocate," or *parakletos* (cf. *1 Jn* 2:1).

ENCYCLICAL, SPE SALVI, NO. 47

SIGN OF HOPE AND COMFORT

On the path of Advent shines the star of Mary Immaculate, "a sign of certain hope and comfort" (*Lumen Gentium,* no. 68). To reach Jesus, the true light, the sun that dispels all the darkness of history, we need light near us, human people who reflect Christ's light and thus illuminate the path to take. And what person is more luminous than Mary? Who can be a better star of hope for us than she, the dawn that announced the day of salvation? (cf. *Spe Salvi,* no. 49). For this reason, the liturgy has us celebrate today, as Christmas approaches, the Solemn Feast of the Immaculate Conception of Mary: the mystery of God's grace that enfolded her from the first instant of her existence as the creature destined to be Mother of the Redeemer, preserving her from the stain of original sin. Looking at her, we recognize the loftiness and beauty of

God's plan for everyone: to become holy and immaculate in love (cf. *Eph* 1:4), in the image of our Creator.

What a great gift to have Mary Immaculate as mother! A mother resplendent with beauty, the transparency of God's love. I am thinking of today's young people, who grow up in an environment saturated with messages that propose false models of happiness. These young men and women risk losing hope because they often seem orphans of true love, which fills life with true meaning and joy. This was a theme dear to my Venerable Predecessor John Paul II, who so often proposed Mary to the youth of our time as the "Mother of Fair Love." Unfortunately, numerous experiences tell us that adolescents, young people, and even children easily fall prey to corrupt love, deceived by unscrupulous adults who, lying to themselves and to them, lure them into the deadends of consumerism; even the most sacred realities, like the human body, a temple of God's love and of life, thus become objects of consumption and this is happening earlier, even in pre-adolescence. How sad it is when youth lose the wonder, the enchantment of the most beautiful sentiments, the value of respect for the body, the manifestation of the person and his unfathomable mystery!

ANGELUS, DECEMBER 8, 2007

THE UNJUSTLY IMPRISONED

The final peroration of *De Consolatione Philosophiae* can be considered a synthesis of the entire teaching that Boethius addressed to himself and all who might find themselves in his same conditions. Thus, in prison he wrote: "So combat vices, dedicate yourselves to a virtuous life oriented by hope, which draws the heart upwards until it reaches Heaven with prayers nourished by humility. Should you refuse to lie, the imposition you have suffered can change into the enormous advantage of always having before your eyes the supreme Judge, who sees and knows how things truly are" (Bk V, 6: *PL* 63, col. 862). Every prisoner, regardless of the reason why he ended up in prison, senses how burdensome this particular human condition is, especially when it is brutalized, as it was for Boethius, by recourse to torture. Then particularly absurd is the condition of those like Boethius — whom the city of Pavia recognizes and celebrates in the liturgy as a martyr of the faith — who are tortured to death for no other reason than their own ideals and political and religious convictions. Boethius, the symbol of an immense number of people unjustly imprisoned in all ages and on all latitudes, is in fact an objective entrance way that gives access to contemplation of the mysterious Crucified One of Golgotha.

GENERAL AUDIENCE ON BOETHIUS AND CASSIODORUS,
MARCH 12, 2008

WITNESS THE MYSTERY

Just as the disciples of Emmaus who, hearts warmed by the Word of the Risen and illuminated by His living presence recognized in the breaking of the bread, without pause returned to Jerusalem and became the proclaimers of Christ's resurrection, we too must take up the path again, animated by the fervent desire to witness the mystery of this love that gives hope to the world.

SYNOD, THE EUCHARIST: SOURCE AND SUMMIT OF THE LIFE AND MISSION OF THE CHURCH, OCTOBER 23, 2005

MADE FOR ETERNITY

God has given himself an "image": in Christ who was made man. In him who was crucified, the denial of false images of God is taken to an extreme. God now reveals his true face in the figure of the sufferer who shares man's God-forsaken condition by taking it upon himself. This innocent sufferer has attained the certitude of hope: there is a God, and God can create justice in a way that we cannot conceive, yet we can begin to grasp it through faith. Yes, there is a resurrection of the flesh (cf. *CCC* 988–1004). There is justice (cf. *ibid.*, 1040). There is an "undoing" of past suffering, a reparation that sets things aright. For this reason, faith in the Last Judgment is first and foremost hope — the need for which was made abundantly clear in the upheavals of recent centuries. I am convinced that the question of justice constitutes the essential argument, or in any case the strongest argument, in favor of faith in eternal life. The purely individual need for a fulfillment that is denied to us in this life, for an everlasting love that we await, is certainly an important motive for believing that man was made for eternity; but only in connection with the impossibility that the injustice of history should be the final word does the necessity for Christ's return and for new life become fully convincing.

To protest against God in the name of justice is not helpful. A world without God is a world without hope (cf. *Eph* 2:12). Only God can create justice. And faith gives us the certainty that he does so.

Encyclical, Spe Salvi, Nos. 43–44

Chapter 3

CHARITY

By charity, we love God above all things
and our neighbor as ourselves for love of
God. Charity, the form of all the virtues,
"binds everything together in perfect
harmony" (*Col* 3:14). (*CCC* 1844)

■

As the Father has loved me, so have I
loved you; abide in my love. If you keep
my commandments, you will abide in
my love, just as I have kept my Father's
commandments and abide in his love. These
things I have spoken to you, that my joy
may be in you, and that your joy may be full.
This is my commandment, that you love one
another as I have loved you. (*Jn* 15:9–12)

Proclaiming the Mystery

In reality, history must run its course, which brings with it
also human dramas and natural calamities. In it a design
of salvation is developed that Christ has already brought
to fulfillment in his Incarnation, death, and Resurrection.

The Church continues to proclaim this mystery and to announce and accomplish it with her preaching, celebration of the sacraments, and witness of charity.

ANGELUS, NOVEMBER 18, 2007

THE HEART OF CHRISTIAN FAITH

"God is love, and he who abides in love abides in God, and God abides in him" (*1 Jn* 4:16). These words from the *First Letter of John* express with remarkable clarity the heart of the Christian faith: the Christian image of God and the resulting image of mankind and its destiny. In the same verse, Saint John also offers a kind of summary of the Christian life: "We have come to know and to believe in the love God has for us."…

In the Church's Liturgy, in her prayer, in the living community of believers, we experience the love of God, we perceive his presence, and we thus learn to recognize that presence in our daily lives.

ENCYCLICAL, DEUS CARITAS EST, NO. 1, 17

THE CENTRALITY OF LOVE

We have come to believe in God's love: in these words the Christian can express the fundamental decision of his life. Being Christian is not the result of an ethical choice or a lofty idea, but the encounter with an event, a person, which gives life a new horizon and a decisive direction. St. John's Gospel describes that event in these words: "God so loved the world that he gave his only Son, that whoever believes in him should ... have eternal life" (3:16). In acknowledging the centrality of love, Christian faith has retained the core of Israel's faith, while at the same time giving it new depth and breadth.

ENCYCLICAL, *DEUS CARITAS EST,* NO. 1

LOVE'S MOST RADICAL FORM

Though up to now we have been speaking mainly of the Old Testament, nevertheless the profound compenetration of the two Testaments as the one Scripture of the Christian faith has already become evident. The real novelty of the New Testament lies not so much in new ideas as in the figure of Christ himself, who gives flesh and blood to those concepts — an unprecedented realism. In the Old Testament, the novelty of the Bible did not consist merely in abstract notions but in God's unpredictable and in some sense unprecedented activity. This divine activity now takes on dramatic form when, in Jesus Christ, it is God himself who goes in search of the "stray sheep," a suffering and lost humanity. When Jesus speaks in his parables of the shepherd who goes after the lost sheep, of the woman who looks for the lost coin, of the father who goes to meet and embrace his prodigal son, these are no mere words: they constitute an explanation of his very being and activity. His death on the Cross is the culmination of that turning of God against himself in which he gives himself in order to raise man up and save him.

This is love in its most radical form. By contemplating the pierced side of Christ (cf. *Jn* 19:37), we can understand the starting-point of this Encyclical Letter: "God is love" (*1 Jn* 4:8). It is there that this truth can be contemplated. It is from there that our definition of love must begin. In this contemplation the Christian discovers the path along which his life and love must move.

Encyclical, Deus Caritas Est, No. 12

Charity and Justice

From this integrally human perspective we can understand more fully the essential role which charity plays in the pursuit of justice. My predecessor, Pope John Paul II, was convinced that justice alone is insufficient to establish truly humane and fraternal relations within society. "In every sphere of interpersonal relationships," he maintained, "justice must, so to speak, be 'corrected' to a considerable extent by that love which, as Saint Paul proclaims, 'is patient and kind' or, in other words, possesses the characteristics of that merciful love which is so much of the essence of the Gospel and Christianity" (*Dives in Misericordia*, 14). Charity, in a word, not only enables justice to become more inventive and to meet new challenges; it also inspires and purifies humanity's efforts to achieve authentic justice and thus the building of a society worthy of man.

Letter, April 28, 2007

Seeing the Father through Jesus

God has made himself visible: in Jesus we are able to see the Father (cf. *Jn* 14:9). Indeed, God is visible in a number of ways. In the love-story recounted by the Bible, he comes towards us, he seeks to win our hearts, all the way to the Last Supper, to the piercing of his heart on the Cross, to his appearances after the Resurrection, and to the great deeds by which, through the activity of the Apostles, he guided the nascent Church along its path. Nor has the Lord been absent from subsequent Church history: he encounters us ever anew, in the men and women who reflect his presence, in his word, in the sacraments, and especially in the Eucharist. In the Church's Liturgy, in her prayer, in the living community of believers, we experience the love of God, we perceive his presence, and we thus learn to recognize that presence in our daily lives. He has loved us first and he continues to do so; we too, then, can respond with love. God does not demand of us a feeling which we ourselves are incapable of producing. He loves us, he makes us see and experience his love, and since he has "loved us first," love can also blossom as a response within us.

ENCYCLICAL, *DEUS CARITAS EST*, NO. 17

Appeal for Peace

I consider it my duty to launch from here a pressing and heartfelt appeal to stop all the armed conflicts which bathe the world in blood. May weapons be silenced and may hatred everywhere give way to love, offense to forgiveness, and discord to union!... We are thinking in particular of the Holy Land, so loved by St. Francis; and of Iraq, Lebanon, and the entire region of the Middle East."

ANGELUS, JUNE 17, 2007

LOVE OF NEIGHBOR

Love of neighbor is thus shown to be possible in the way proclaimed by the Bible, by Jesus. It consists in the very fact that, in God and with God, I love even the person whom I do not like or even know. This can only take place on the basis of an intimate encounter with God, an encounter which has become a communion of will, even affecting my feelings. Then I learn to look on this other person not simply with my eyes and my feelings, but from the perspective of Jesus Christ. His friend is my friend. Going beyond exterior appearances, I perceive in others an interior desire for a sign of love, of concern. This I can offer them not only through the organizations intended for such purposes, accepting it perhaps as a political necessity. Seeing with the eyes of Christ, I can give to others much more than their outward necessities; I can give them the look of love which they crave.

ENCYCLICAL, *DEUS CARITAS EST,* No. 18

OFFER IT UP

I would like to add here another brief comment with some relevance for everyday living. There used to be a form of devotion — perhaps less practiced today but quite wide-spread not long ago — that included the idea of "offering up" the minor daily hardships that continually strike at us like irritating "jabs," thereby giving them a meaning. Of course, there were some exaggerations and perhaps un-healthy applications of this devotion, but we need to ask ourselves whether there may not after all have been some-thing essential and helpful contained within it. What does it mean to offer something up? Those who did so were convinced that they could insert these little annoyances into Christ's great "compassion" so that they somehow be-came part of the treasury of compassion so greatly needed by the human race. In this way, even the small inconve-niences of daily life could acquire meaning and contribute to the economy of good and of human love. Maybe we should consider whether it might be judicious to revive this practice ourselves.

ENCYCLICAL, *SPE SALVI*, NO. 40

ARMOR OF LIGHT

In every sick person, whoever he or she may be, may you be able to recognize and serve Christ himself; make them perceive with your acts and words the signs of his merciful love. To carry out this "mission" well, endeavor, as St. Paul instructs us, to "put on the armor of light" (*Rom* 13:12), which consists in the Word of God, the gifts of the Spirit, the grace of the Sacraments, the theological and cardinal virtues; fight evil and abandon sin that darkens our life....

[L]et us renew our good resolutions of evangelical life. "It is full time now for you to wake from sleep" (*Rom* 13:11), the Apostle urges; it is time to convert, to throw off the lethargy of sin, to prepare ourselves confidently to welcome "the Lord who comes."

HOMILY, DECEMBER 2, 2007

SEEING THE TRINITY

"If you see charity, you see the Trinity," wrote Saint Augustine (*De Trinitate*, VIII, 8, 12: CCL 50, 287). In the foregoing reflections, we have been able to focus our attention on the Pierced one (cf. *Jn* 19:37, *Zech* 12:10), recognizing the plan of the Father who, moved by love (cf. *Jn* 3:16), sent his only-begotten Son into the world to redeem man. By dying on the Cross — as Saint John tells us — Jesus "gave up his Spirit" (*Jn* 19:30), anticipating the gift of the Holy Spirit that he would make after his Resurrection (cf. *Jn* 20:22). This was to fulfill the promise of "rivers of living water" that would flow out of the hearts of believers, through the outpouring of the Spirit (cf. *Jn* 7:38–39). The Spirit, in fact, is that interior power which harmonizes their hearts with Christ's heart and moves them to love their brethren as Christ loved them, when he bent down to wash the feet of the disciples (cf. *Jn* 13:1–13), and above all when he gave his life for us (cf. *Jn* 13:1, 15:13).

ENCYCLICAL, DEUS CARITAS EST, No. 19

Authentic Commitment

In practice our ecumenical and interreligious sensitivity must always be built on the local Catholic Churches' involvement with the most cordial appreciation of the different ritual expressions.

Then, recalling the words of St. Paul: "So neither he who plants nor he who waters is anything, but only God who gives the growth" (1 *Cor* 3:7), may we always glimpse through prayer the true source of commitment in charity, and by it verify its authenticity.

The same Apostle's admonition is clear: "Let each man take care how he builds upon it. For no other foundation can any one lay than that which is laid, which is Jesus Christ" (1 *Cor* 3:10–11).

Being rooted in the Eucharist is indispensable to our work. The future scope of ecclesial charity must be based on the "Eucharistic measure": only what does not contradict, but rather finds and draws nourishment from the mystery of Eucharistic love and by the vision of the cosmos, man, and history that flows from it, can guarantee the authenticity of our giving and provide us with a sure foundation on which to build.

ADDRESS, JUNE 21, 2007

Church Must Practice Love

Love of neighbor, grounded in the love of God, is first and foremost a responsibility for each individual member of the faithful, but it is also a responsibility for the entire ecclesial community at every level: from the local community to the particular Church and to the Church universal in its entirety. As a community, the Church must practice love. Love thus needs to be organized if it is to be an ordered service to the community. The awareness of this responsibility has had a constitutive relevance in the Church from the beginning: "All who believed were together and had all things in common; and they sold their possessions and goods and distributed them to all, as any had need" (*Acts* 2:44–45). In these words, Saint Luke provides a kind of definition of the Church, whose constitutive elements include fidelity to the "teaching of the Apostles," "communion" (*koinonia*), "the breaking of the bread," and "prayer" (cf. *Acts* 2:42).

ENCYCLICAL, DEUS CARITAS EST, NO. 20

AN ESSENTIAL ACTIVITY

As the years went by and the Church spread further afield, the exercise of charity became established as one of her essential activities, along with the administration of the sacraments and the proclamation of the word: love for widows and orphans, prisoners, and the sick and needy of every kind, is as essential to her as the ministry of the sacraments and preaching of the Gospel. The Church cannot neglect the service of charity any more than she can neglect the Sacraments and the Word.

ENCYCLICAL, DEUS CARITAS EST, NO. 22

Artisans of the Civilization of Love

Dear friends, may these days of work and listening be fruitful for all. I address my prayers to Eternal God for this, so that he may pour out upon each one of the participants in the meeting an abundance of his Blessings, wisdom, and love. May he free human hearts of all hatred and uproot all violence, and make us all artisans of the civilization of love.

Greeting, October 21, 2007

Doing Good to All

Thus far, two essential facts have emerged from our reflections:

a) The Church's deepest nature is expressed in her three-fold responsibility: of proclaiming the word of God (*kerygma-martyria*), celebrating the sacraments (*leitourgia*), and exercising the ministry of charity (*diakonia*). These duties presuppose each other and are inseparable. For the Church, charity is not a kind of welfare activity which could equally well be left to others, but is a part of her nature, an indispensable expression of her very being. (Cf. Congregation for Bishops, Directory for the Pastoral Ministry of Bishops *Apostolorum Successores* [22 February 2004], 194, Vatican City 2004, p. 213.)

b) The Church is God's family in the world. In this family no one ought to go without the necessities of life. Yet at the same time *caritas-agape* extends beyond the frontiers of the Church. The parable of the Good Samaritan remains as a standard which imposes universal love towards the needy whom we encounter "by chance" (cf. *Lk* 10:31), whoever they may be. Without in any way detracting from this commandment of universal love, the Church also has a specific responsibility: within the ecclesial family no member should suffer through being in need. The teaching of the *Letter to the Galatians* is emphatic: "So then, as we have opportunity, let us do good to all men, and especially to those who are of the household of faith" (6:10).

Encyclical, Deus Caritas Est, No. 25

Love for the Poor

Love for the poor and the divine liturgy go hand in hand, love for the poor is liturgy. The two horizons are present in every liturgy that is celebrated and experienced in the Church which, by her nature, is opposed to any separation between worship and life, between faith and works, between prayer and charity for the brethren.

Audience, October 1, 2008

Remaining Close with Those in Need

We do not need a State which regulates and controls everything, but a State which, in accordance with the principle of subsidiarity, generously acknowledges and supports initiatives arising from the different social forces and combines spontaneity with closeness to those in need. The Church is one of those living forces: she is alive with the love enkindled by the Spirit of Christ. This love does not simply offer people material help, but refreshment and care for their souls, something which often is even more necessary than material support. In the end, the claim that just social structures would make works of charity super-fluous masks a materialist conception of man: the mistaken notion that man can live "by bread alone" (*Mt* 4:4; cf. *Dt* 8:3) — a conviction that demeans man and ultimately disregards all that is specifically human.

ENCYCLICAL, DEUS CARITAS EST, NO. 28

OMNIPOTENCE OF CHRIST'S LOVE

Christ triumphed over death with the omnipotence of his love. Love alone is omnipotent. This love impelled Christ to die for us and thus to overcome death. Yes, love alone gives access to the Kingdom of life!

HOMILY, AUGUST 15, 2008

THE GOOD SAMARITAN'S EXAMPLE

Following the example given in the parable of the Good Samaritan, Christian charity is first of all the simple re-sponse to immediate needs and specific situations: feeding the hungry, clothing the naked, caring for and healing the sick, visiting those in prison, etc. The Church's charitable organizations, beginning with those of *Caritas* (at diocesan, national, and international levels), ought to do everything in their power to provide the resources and above all the personnel needed for this work. Individuals who care for those in need must first be professionally competent: they should be properly trained in what to do and how to do it, and committed to continuing care. Yet, while professional competence is a primary, fundamental requirement, it is not of itself sufficient. We are dealing with human beings, and human beings always need something more than technically proper care. They need humanity. They need heartfelt concern. Those who work for the Church's charitable organizations must be distinguished by the fact that they do not merely meet the needs of the moment, but they dedicate themselves to others with heartfelt concern, enabling them to experience the richness of their humanity. Consequently, in addition to their necessary professional training, these charity workers need a "formation of the heart": they need to be led to that encounter with God in Christ which awakens their love and opens their spirits to others. As a result, love of neighbor will no longer be for them a commandment imposed, so to speak, from without, but a consequence deriving from their faith, a faith which becomes active through love (cf. *Gal* 5:6).

ENCYCLICAL, *DEUS CARITAS EST*, NO. 31

MARRIAGE AS INSTRUMENT OF SALVATION

God's gift to us of marriage and family life enables us to experience something of the infinite love that unites the three divine persons: Father, Son, and Holy Spirit. Human beings, made in the image and likeness of God, are made for love; indeed at the core of our being, we long to love and to be loved in return. Marriage is truly an instrument of salvation, not only for married people but for the whole of society. Like any truly worthwhile goal, it places demands upon us, it challenges us, it calls us to be prepared to sacrifice our own interests for the good of the other. It requires us to exercise tolerance and to offer forgiveness. It invites us to nurture and protect the gift of new life.... I encourage all of you in your efforts to promote a proper understanding and appreciation of the inestimable good that marriage and family life offer to human society.

GENERAL ADDRESS, MAY 5, 2010

HUMILITY THROUGH SERVING

This proper way of serving others also leads to humility. The one who serves does not consider himself superior to the one served, however miserable his situation at the moment may be. Christ took the lowest place in the world — the Cross — and by this radical humility he redeemed us and constantly comes to our aid. Those who are in a position to help others will realize that in doing so they themselves receive help; being able to help others is no merit or achievement of their own. This duty is a grace. The more we do for others, the more we understand and can appropriate the words of Christ: "We are unworthy servants" (*Lk* 17:10). We recognize that we are not acting on the basis of any superiority or greater personal efficiency, but because the Lord has graciously enabled us to do so.

ENCYCLICAL, *DEUS CARITAS EST,* No. 35

PART TWO

THE CARDINAL
VIRTUES

PRUDENCE, JUSTICE, FORTITUDE, AND TEMPERANCE

Four virtues play a pivotal role and
accordingly are called "cardinal";
all the others are grouped around them.
They are: prudence, justice, fortitude, and
temperance. "If anyone loves righteousness,
[Wisdom's] labors are virtues; for she
teaches temperance and prudence, justice,
and courage" (*Wis* 8:7). These virtues
are praised under other names in many
passages of Scripture. (*CCC* 1805)

■

The human virtues are stable dispositions
of the intellect and the will that govern
our acts, order our passions, and guide our
conduct in accordance with reason and
faith. They can be grouped around the
four cardinal virtues: prudence, justice,
fortitude, and temperance. (*CCC* 1834)

■

And if any one loves righteousness,
her [Wisdom's] labors are virtues; for she
teaches self-control and prudence, justice
and courage." (*Wis* 8:7)

Human Virtues
Human virtues are firm attitudes, stable dispositions, habitual perfections of intellect and will that govern our actions, order our passions, and guide our conduct according to reason and faith. They make possible ease, self-mastery, and joy in leading a morally good life. The virtuous man is he who freely practices the good.

The moral virtues are acquired by human effort. They are the fruit and seed of morally good acts; they dispose all the powers of the human being for communion with divine love.

CCC 1804

The Cardinal Virtues
Prudence is the virtue that disposes practical reason to discern our true good in every circumstance and to choose the right means of achieving it; "the prudent man looks where he is going" (*Prov* 14:15). "Keep sane and sober for your prayers" (1 *Pet* 4:7). Prudence is "right reason in action," writes St. Thomas Aquinas, following Aristotle (St. Thomas Aquinas, *STh* II-II, 47, 2). It is not to be confused with timidity or fear, nor with duplicity or dissimulation. It is called *auriga virtutum* (the charioteer of the virtues); it guides the other virtues by setting rule and measure. It is prudence that immediately guides the judgment of conscience. The prudent man determines and directs his conduct in accordance with this judgment. With the help of this virtue we apply moral principles to particular cases without error and overcome doubts about the good to achieve and the evil to avoid.

Justice is the moral virtue that consists in the constant and firm will to give their due to God and neighbor. Justice toward God is called the "virtue of religion." Justice toward men disposes one to respect the rights of each and to establish in human relationships the harmony that promotes equity with regard to persons and to the common good. The just man, often mentioned in the Sacred Scriptures, is distinguished by habitual right thinking and the uprightness of his conduct toward his neighbor. "You shall not be partial to the poor or defer to the great, but in righteousness shall you judge your neighbor" (*Lev* 19:15). "Masters, treat your slaves justly and fairly, knowing that you also have a Master in heaven" (*Col* 4:1).

Fortitude is the moral virtue that ensures firmness in difficulties and constancy in the pursuit of the good. It strengthens the resolve to resist temptations and to overcome obstacles in the moral life. The virtue of fortitude enables one to conquer fear, even fear of death, and to face trials and persecutions. It disposes one even to renounce and sacrifice his life in defense of a just cause. "The Lord is my strength and my song" (*Ps* 118:14). "In the world you have tribulation; but be of good cheer, I have overcome the world" (*Jn* 16:33).

Temperance is the moral virtue that moderates the attraction of pleasures and provides balance in the use of created goods. It ensures the will's mastery over instincts and keeps desires within the limits of what is honorable. The temperate person directs the sensitive appetites toward what is good and maintains a healthy discretion: "Do not follow your inclination and strength, walking according to the desires of your heart" (*Sir* 5:2; cf. 37:27–31). Temperance is often praised in the Old Testament: "Do not follow your base desires, but restrain your appetites" (*Sir* 18:30). In the New Testament it is called "moderation" or "sobriety." We ought "to live sober, upright, and godly lives in this world" (*Titus* 2:12).

> To live well is nothing other than to love God with all one's heart, with all one's soul and with all one's efforts; from this it comes about that love is kept whole and uncorrupted (through temperance). No misfortune can disturb it (and this is fortitude). It obeys only (God) (and this is justice), and is careful in discerning things, so as not to be surprised by deceit or trickery (and this is prudence). (St. Augustine, *De moribus eccl.* 1, 25, 46: PL 32, 1330–1331)
>
> *CCC* 1806–1809

The Virtues and Grace

Human virtues acquired by education, by deliberate acts and by a perseverance ever-renewed in repeated efforts are purified and elevated by divine grace. With God's help, they forge character and give facility in the practice of the good. The virtuous man is happy to practice them.

It is not easy for man, wounded by sin, to maintain moral balance. Christ's gift of salvation offers us the grace necessary to persevere in the pursuit of the virtues. Everyone should always ask for this grace of light and strength, frequent the sacraments, cooperate with the Holy Spirit, and follow his calls to love what is good and shun evil.

CCC 1810-1811

The Wealth of the People of God

The person who has recognized Christ as Wisdom Incarnate and for his sake has left everything else becomes a "peacemaker," both in the Christian community and in the world. In other words, he becomes a seed of the Kingdom of God that is already present and growing towards its full manifestation.

Therefore, in the perspective of the two words, "Wisdom-Christ," the Word of God offers us a complete vision of man in history: fascinated by Wisdom, he seeks it and finds it in Christ, leaving everything for him and receiving in exchange the priceless gift of the Kingdom of God; and clothed in temperance, prudence, justice, and strength — the "cardinal" virtues — he lives the witness of charity in the Church.

One might wonder whether this perception of the human being can also constitute an ideal of life for the people of our time, especially for the young. That this is possible is shown by countless personal and community testimonies of Christian life which still constitute the wealth of the People of God, pilgrims through history.

Homily, May 6, 2006

Chapter 4

PRUDENCE

Prudence disposes the practical reason to
discern, in every circumstance, our true
good and to choose the right means for
achieving it. (*CCC* 1835)

∎

And if any one loves righteousness,
her [Wisdom's] labors are virtues; for
she teaches self-control and prudence,
justice and courage; nothing in life is
more profitable for men than these.
(*Wis* 8:7)

Search for the Truth

The first characteristic which the Lord requires of his servant
is fidelity. He has been entrusted with a great good that
does not belong to him. The Church is not our Church
but his Church, the Church of God. The servant must
account for how he has managed the good that has been
entrusted to him....

The second characteristic that Jesus asks of the servant is prudence. Here it is necessary first to eliminate a misunderstanding. Prudence is something other than shrewdness. Prudence, according to the Greek philosophical tradition, is the first of the cardinal virtues. It indicates the primacy of the truth which, through "prudence," becomes a criterion for our action. Prudence demands humble, disciplined, and watchful reason that does not let itself be blinded by prejudices; it does not judge according to desires and passions but rather seeks the truth, even though it may prove uncomfortable. Prudence means searching for the truth and acting in conformity with it. The prudent servant is first and foremost a man of truth and a man of sincere reason. God, through Jesus Christ, has opened wide for us the window of the truth which, before our own mere forces, often remains narrow and only partially transparent. In Sacred Scripture and in faith in the Church God shows us the essential truth about man, which impresses the right orientation upon our action. Thus, the first cardinal virtue of the priest as minister of Jesus Christ consists in letting himself be molded by the truth that Christ shows us. In this way we become truly reasonable people, who judge on the basis of the whole and not on chance details. Let us not allow ourselves to be guided by what we see through the small window of our personal astuteness, but, rather, let us look at the world and at human beings through the large window that Christ has opened to us on the whole truth and thus recognize what truly counts in life.

HOMILY, SEPTEMBER 12, 2009

CARE IN TRAVEL

For countries in the northern hemisphere the end of June marks the beginning of the summer season and, for many, the beginning of vacations. I hope that everyone will be able to live serenely a few days of well-earned rest and relaxation, and I would like to address an appeal for prudence to those who are setting out for their various vacation sites. Every day, unfortunately, especially on the weekend, road accidents are recorded with so many human lives tragically cut short, and more than half the victims are young people.

In recent years much has been done to prevent these tragic events but more can and must be done, with the contribution and involvement of all. It is necessary to combat distraction and superficiality which, in an instant, can ruin one's own future and that of others. Life is precious and unique: it must always be respected and protected, also by proper and careful conduct on the roads.

May the Virgin Mary, who accompanies us on our daily journey through life, watch over travelers and obtain mercy for road victims. With the upcoming Feast of the Holy Apostles Peter and Paul, let us entrust the Church and her missionary action throughout the world to Her, the heavenly Queen of the Apostles.

ANGELUS, JUNE 26, 2005

SOLIDARITY OF ALL PEOPLE

The just care of immigrants and the building up of a solidarity of labor (cf. *Laborem Exercens,* 8) requires governments, humanitarian agencies, peoples of faith, and all
citizens to cooperate with prudence and patient deter-
mination. Domestic and international policies aimed at
regulating immigration must be based on criteria of equity
and balance, and particular care is needed to facilitate the
reunification of families. At the same time, conditions that
foster increased work opportunities in peoples' places of
origin are to be promoted as far as possible (cf. *Gaudium
et Spes,* 66).

ADDRESS, OCTOBER 27, 2008

PRIESTS CALLED TO BE HUMAN

As the first point, therefore, the priest must be on God's
side. Only in Christ is this need, this prerequisite of mediation fully brought about. This Mystery was therefore
necessary: the Son of God is made man so that he may be
the true bridge for us, the true mediation....

The other element is that the priest must be man, human in all senses. That is, he must live true humanity, true
humanism; he must be educated, have a human formation, human virtues; he must develop his intelligence, his
will, his sentiments, his affections; he must be a true man,
a man according to the will of the Creator, of the Redeemer, for we know that the human being is wounded and the
question of "what man is" is obscured by the event of sin

that hurt human nature even to the quick. Thus people say: "he lied" "it is human"; "he stole" "it is human"; but this is not really being human. Human means being generous, being good, being a just person, it means true prudence and wisdom. Therefore emerging with Christ's help from this dark area in our nature so as to succeed in being truly human in the image of God is a lifelong process that must begin in our training for the priesthood. It must subsequently be achieved, however, and continue as long as we live. I think that basically these two things go hand in hand: being of God and with God and being true man, in the true sense meant by the Creator when he formed this creature that we are.

Lectio Divina, February 18, 2010

Peace among Peoples

Thus I would now like to join with the Presidents of both countries' gratitude and joy in the special celebration of this historical date. They are grateful for the work of my Predecessor who so distinguished himself during his long Pontificate for promoting concord among all peoples. This success, causing a pleasant and unexpected surprise in the world, is an example of how, in the face of any controversy, it is always necessary to overcome discouragement and not to abandon the process of patient dialogue and negotiation, conducted with wisdom and prudence, in order to reach a just and worthy solution by peaceful means proper to civilized peoples, especially when their members know that they are also brothers and sisters, children of one God and Father.

Recent history, with the experience of various fatally failed attempts and drastic solutions which in controversies in various parts of the world have given rise to very grave consequences, helps us to discover the horrors which that Papal intervention spared the Argentine and Chilean peoples, as well as other nations in the region. And today's reality, with the abundant positive results of mutual collaboration between the two countries and which are an exemplary and undeniable proof of the fruits of peace, began to emerge precisely thirty years ago.

LETTER TO THE PRESIDENTS OF ARGENTINA AND CHILE,
NOVEMBER 29, 2008

CARING FOR THE ENVIRONMENT

Our Christian faith teaches that God the Creator made all things good (cf. *Gn* 1); and gave the earth to us humans to cultivate and take care of as stewards (cf. *Gn* 2:15). We observe that many human beings, at all levels, have continued to abuse nature and destroy God's beautiful world by exploitation of natural resources beyond what is sustainable and useful. There is an irresponsible degradation and senseless destruction of the earth, which is "our mother."

In complicity with those who exercise political and economic leadership in Africa, some businesses, governments, and multinational and transnational companies engage in business that pollute the environment, destroy flora and fauna, thus causing unprecedented erosion and desertification of large areas of arable land. All of these threaten the survival of mankind and the entire eco-system. This has raised among scientists and stakeholders the awareness of the deleterious effects of climate change, global warming, natural calamities (like earthquakes, sea-quakes, and their consequences like tsunami).

To make the earth habitable beyond the present generation and to guarantee sustainable and responsible care of the earth, we call upon the particular Churches to:

- promote environmental education and awareness;
- persuade their local and national governments to adopt policies and binding legal regulations for the protection of the environment and promote alternative and renewable sources of energy; and
- encourage all to plant trees and treat nature and its resources, respecting the common good and the integrity of nature, with transparency and respect for human dignity.

THE CHURCH IN AFRICA IN SERVICE TO RECONCILIATION, JUSTICE AND PEACE, OCTOBER 24, 2009

INSTRUCTION TO NEW BISHOPS

Serenity in relationships, sensitive treatment, and simplicity of life are gifts that certainly enrich the human personality of the Bishop.

In his Book of *Pastoral Rule*, St. Gregory the Great wrote that "the government of souls is the art of arts" (Part I, Chapter I).

It is an art that requires the constant growth of the virtues, among which I would like to recall prudence, which St. Bernard described as "the mother of strength." Prudence will make you patient with yourselves and with others, courageous and firm in your decisions, merciful and just, concerned solely with your salvation and the salvation of your brethren "with fear and trembling" (cf. *Phil* 2:12).

The total gift of yourselves, which the care of the Lord's flock requires, needs the support of an intense spiritual life, nourished by persevering personal and community prayer. Constant contact with God should therefore mark your days and accompany your every activity.

Living in intimate union with Christ will help you to achieve that necessary balance between inner recollection and the necessary effort required by the many occupations of life, avoiding exaggerated activism.

On the day of your episcopal consecration you promised to pray tirelessly for your people. Dear Brothers, always stay faithful to this commitment, which will enable you to exercise your pastoral ministry irreproachably.

Through prayer, the doors of your hearts are opened to God's plan, which is a plan of love to which he has called you by uniting you very closely with Christ through the grace of the episcopate. Following him, Shepherd and Guardian of your souls (cf. 1 *Pet* 2:25), you will be impelled to strive for holiness without tiring, which is the fundamental goal of every Christian's life.

ADDRESS, SEPTEMBER 21, 2006

Responding to God's Call

To respond to the Lord's call means facing in prudence and simplicity every danger and even persecutions, since "a disciple is not above his teacher, nor a servant above his master" (*Mt* 10:24). Having become one with their Master, the disciples are no longer alone as they announce the Kingdom of heaven; Jesus himself is acting in them: "He who receives you receives me, and he who receives me receives him who sent me" (*Mt* 10:40). Furthermore, as true witnesses, "clothed with power from on high" (*Lk* 24:49), they preach "repentance and the forgiveness of sins" (*Lk* 24:47) to all peoples.

Message, April 13, 2008

Preach as True Witnesses

The promises made to our fathers were fulfilled entirely in Jesus Christ. In this regard, the Second Vatican Council says: "The Son, therefore, came, sent by the Father. It was in him, before the foundation of the world, that the Father chose us and predestined us to become adopted sons.... To carry out the will of the Father, Christ inaugurated the kingdom of heaven on earth and revealed to us the mystery of that kingdom. By his obedience he brought about redemption" (Dogmatic Constitution *Lumen Gentium*, 3). And Jesus already in his public life, while preaching in Galilee, chose some disciples to be his close collaborators in the messianic ministry. For example, on the occasion of the multiplication of the loaves, he said to the Apostles: "You give them something to eat" (*Mt* 14:16), encouraging them to assume the needs of the crowds to whom he wished to offer nourishment, but also to reveal the food "which endures to eternal life" (*Jn* 6:27). He was moved to compassion for the people, because while visiting cities and villages, he found the crowds weary and helpless, like sheep without a shepherd (cf. *Mt* 9:36). From this gaze of love came the invitation to his disciples: "Pray therefore the Lord of the harvest to send out laborers into his harvest" (*Mt* 9:38), and he sent the Twelve initially "to the lost sheep of the house of Israel" with precise instructions. If we pause to meditate on this passage of Matthew's Gospel, commonly called the "missionary discourse," we may take note of those aspects which distinguish the missionary activity of a Christian community, eager to remain faithful to the example and teaching of Jesus. To respond to the Lord's call means facing in prudence and simplicity every danger and even persecutions, since "a disciple is not above his teacher, nor a servant above his master" (*Mt* 10:24). Having become one with their Master, the disciples are no longer alone as they announce the Kingdom of heaven; Jesus himself is acting in them: "He who receives you receives me, and he who receives me receives him who sent me" (*Mt* 10:40). Furthermore, as true witnesses, "clothed with power from on high" (*Lk* 24:49), they preach "repentance and the forgiveness of sins" (*Lk* 24:47) to all peoples.

MESSAGE, APRIL 13, 2008

EDUCATION OF CHILDREN WITH MEDIA

Media education should be positive. Children exposed to what is aesthetically and morally excellent are helped to develop appreciation, prudence, and the skills of discernment. Here it is important to recognize the fundamental value of parents' example and the benefits of introducing young people to children's classics in literature, to the fine arts, and to uplifting music. While popular literature will always have its place in culture, the temptation to sensationalize should not be passively accepted in places of learning. Beauty, a kind of mirror of the divine, inspires and vivifies young hearts and minds, while ugliness and coarseness have a depressing impact on attitudes and behavior.

Like education in general, media education requires formation in the exercise of freedom. This is a demanding task. So often freedom is presented as a relentless search for pleasure or new experiences. Yet this is a condemnation not a liberation! True freedom could never condemn the individual — especially a child — to an insatiable quest for novelty. In the light of truth, authentic freedom is experienced as a definitive response to God's "yes" to humanity, calling us to choose, not indiscriminately but deliberately, all that is good, true, and beautiful. Parents, then, as the guardians of that freedom, while gradually giving their children greater freedom, introduce them to the profound joy of life (cf. Address to the Fifth World Meeting of Families, Valencia, 8 July 2006).

MESSAGE, MAY 22, 2009

Chapter 5

JUSTICE

**Justice consists in the firm and constant
will to give God and neighbor their due.
(*CCC* 1836)**

■

**To do righteousness and justice is more
acceptable to the LORD than sacrifice....
When justice is done, it is a joy to the
righteous, but dismay to evildoers.
(*Prov* 21:3, 15)**

REDUCING SUFFERING

Like action, suffering is a part of our human existence.
Suffering stems partly from our finitude and partly from
the mass of sin which has accumulated over the course of
history and continues to grow unabated today. Certainly
we must do whatever we can to reduce suffering: to avoid
as far as possible the suffering of the innocent; to soothe
pain; to give assistance in overcoming mental suffering.
These are obligations both in justice and in love, and they
are included among the fundamental requirements of the

Christian life and every truly human life. Great progress has been made in the battle against physical pain; yet the sufferings of the innocent, and mental suffering have, if anything, increased in recent decades. Indeed, we must do all we can to overcome suffering, but to banish it from the world altogether is not in our power. This is simply because we are unable to shake off our finitude, and because none of us is capable of eliminating the power of evil, of sin which, as we plainly see, is a constant source of suffering. Only God is able to do this: only a God who personally enters history by making himself man and suffering within history. We know that this God exists, and hence that this power to "take away the sin of the world" (cf. *Jn* 1:29) is present in the world. Through faith in the existence of this power, hope for the world's healing has emerged in history. It is, however, hope — not yet fulfillment; hope that gives us the courage to place ourselves on the side of good even in seemingly hopeless situations, aware that, as far as the external course of history is concerned, the power of sin will continue to be a terrible presence.

ENCYCLICAL, *SPE SALVI,* NO. 36

PROMOTING HUMAN DIGNITY

To meet these challenges, only love for neighbor can inspire within us justice at the service of life and the promotion of human dignity. Only love within the family, founded on a man and a woman, who are created in the image of God, can assure that inter-generational solidarity which transmits love and justice to future generations. Only charity can encourage us to place the human person once more at the center of life in society and at the center of a globalized world governed by justice.

LETTER, APRIL 28, 2007

COOPERATION BETWEEN CHURCH AND STATE

The Church is equally convinced that State and religion are called to support each other as they together serve the personal and social well-being of all (cf. *Gaudium et Spes*, 76). This harmonious cooperation between Church and State requires ecclesial and civic leaders to carry out their public duties with undaunted concern for the common good. By cultivating a spirit of honesty and impartiality, and by keeping justice their aim, civil and ecclesial leaders earn the trust of the people and enhance a sense of the shared responsibility of all citizens to promote a civilization of love. All should be motivated by the desire to serve rather than to gain personally or to benefit a privileged few. Everyone shares in the task of strengthening public institutions so as to safeguard them from the corruption of factionalism and elitism. In this regard, it is encouraging to see the many initiatives undertaken at various levels of Filipino society to protect the weak, especially the unborn, the sick, and the elderly.

ADDRESS, OCTOBER 27, 2008

ANIMATED BY THE HOLY SPIRIT

The entire Church, as beloved Pope John Paul II used to say, is one great movement animated by the Holy Spirit, a river that travels through history to irrigate it with God's grace and make it full of life, goodness, beauty, justice, and peace.

REGINA CAELI, JUNE 4, 2006

AUTHENTIC GENEROSITY

Today, in the First Reading, the Prophet Amos speaks of the same fundamental decision to be made day by day. Using strong words, he stigmatizes a lifestyle typical of those who allow themselves to be absorbed by a selfish quest for profit in every possible form and which is expressed in the thirst for gain, contempt for the poor and their exploitation, to one's own advantage (cf. Amos 8:5). The Christian must energetically reject all this, opening his heart on the contrary to sentiments of authentic generosity. It must be generosity which, as the Apostle Paul exhorts in the Second Reading, is expressed in sincere love for all and is manifested in prayer. Actually, praying for others is a great act of charity. The Apostle invites us in the first place to pray for those who have tasks of responsibility in the civil community because, he explains, if they aspire to do good, positive consequences derive from their decisions, assuring peace and "a quiet and peaceable life, godly and respectful in every way" (1 *Tim* 2:2). Thus, may our prayer never be lacking, a spiritual contribution to building an

Ecclesial Community that is faithful to Christ and to the construction of a society in which there is greater justice and solidarity.

HOMILY, SEPTEMBER 23, 2007

SUFFERING FOR OTHERS

Furthermore, the capacity to accept suffering for the sake of goodness, truth, and justice is an essential criterion of humanity, because if my own well-being and safety are ultimately more important than truth and justice, then the power of the stronger prevails, then violence and untruth reign supreme. Truth and justice must stand above my comfort and physical well-being, or else my life itself becomes a lie. In the end, even the "yes" to love is a source of suffering, because love always requires expropriations of my "I," in which I allow myself to be pruned and wounded. Love simply cannot exist without this painful renunciation of myself, for otherwise it becomes pure selfishness and thereby ceases to be love.

ENCYCLICAL, SPE SALVI, NO. 38

FORGIVENESS PERFECTS JUSTICE

Forgiveness leads people towards a deeper and richer humanity, awakening in each one the best of himself or herself. But this attitude that helps men and women develop is necessarily associated with the demands of justice. Forgiveness is not a sign of weakness, and they cannot ignore the legitimate claims of the victims of injustice, who are asking that their rights be recognized and reparation made for the damage caused to them.

Forgiveness is, in a certain way, the perfecting of the frail and imperfect human justice, making it possible to heal the wounds that have sometimes permanently marked people in their very depths and to re-establish in the best possible way the human relations that have been destabilized.

To defend the sacred value of the human person and encourage respect for others and for religious freedom, it is necessary, therefore, that the spirit of reconciliation and justice be inculcated in the young generations, especially in the family and in education. Societies will thus be able to progress in solidarity and brotherhood, so that violence may no longer be advocated as a solution to the problems that confront them and so that religion may never be used to justify such a decision nor to create inequalities between people.

ADDRESS, DECEMBER 1, 2005

TRUTH AND LOVE

The Christian faith has shown us that truth, justice, and love are not simply ideals, but enormously weighty realities. It has shown us that God — Truth and Love in person — desired to suffer for us and with us.

ENCYCLICAL, *SPE SALVI*, NO. 39

THE TRUTH OF PEACE

The Pastoral Constitution *Gaudium et Spes*, promulgated forty years ago at the conclusion of the Second Vatican Council, stated that mankind will not succeed in "building a truly more human world for everyone, everywhere on earth, unless all people are renewed in spirit and converted to the truth of peace" (No. 77). But what do those words, "the truth of peace," really mean? To respond adequately to this question, we must realize that peace cannot be reduced to the simple absence of armed conflict, but needs to be understood as "the fruit of an order which has been planted in human society by its divine Founder," an order "which must be brought about by humanity in its thirst for ever more perfect justice" (*Ibid.*, 78). As the result of an order planned and willed by the love of God, peace has an intrinsic and invincible truth of its own and corresponds "to an irrepressible yearning and hope dwelling within us" (John Paul II, *Message for the 2004 World Day of Peace*, 9).

Seen in this way, peace appears as a heavenly gift and a divine grace which demands at every level the exercise of the highest responsibility: that of conforming human history — in truth, justice, freedom, and love — to the divine order.

MESSAGE, JANUARY 1, 2006

THIRST FOR JUSTICE

Christ's Gospel responds positively to Man's thirst for justice, but in an unexpected and surprising way. He does not propose a social or political revolution but rather one of love, which he has already brought about with his Cross and his Resurrection. It is on these that are founded the Beatitudes which present a new horizon of justice, unveiled at Easter, thanks to which we can become just and build a better world.

ANGELUS, FEBRUARY 14, 2010

GRACE IN JUSTICE

God is justice and creates justice. This is our consolation and our hope. And in his justice there is also grace. This we know by turning our gaze to the crucified and risen Christ. Both these things — justice and grace — must be seen in their correct inner relationship. Grace does not cancel out justice. It does not make wrong into right. It is not a sponge which wipes everything away, so that whatever someone has done on earth ends up being of equal value.

ENCYCLICAL, *SPE SALVI*, NO. 44

The Gift of Reconciliation

How important and, unfortunately, insufficiently under-stood is the gift of Reconciliation which sets hearts at rest! Christ's peace is only spread through the renewed hearts of reconciled men and women who have made themselves servants of justice, ready to spread peace in the world with the force of the truth alone, without descending to com-promises with the world's mentality because the world cannot give Christ's peace: this is how the Church can be the leaven of that reconciliation which comes from God. She can only be so if she remains docile to the Spirit and bears witness to the Gospel, only if she carries the Cross like Jesus and with Jesus. The saints of every epoch witness precisely to this!

In the light of this word of life, dear brothers and sisters, may the prayer we are raising to God in spiritual union with the Virgin Mary become ever more fervent and intense. May the Virgin of listening, the Mother of the Church, obtain for our communities and for all Christians a renewed outpouring of the Holy Spirit, the Paraclete. *"Emitte Spiritum tuum et creabuntur, et renovabis faciem terrae* — Send forth your Spirit, and they shall be recre-ated, and you shall renew the face of the earth." Amen.

HOMILY, MAY 11, 2008

Light of the World

Today's Solemnity can offer us this perspective, based on the manifestation of a God who revealed himself

in history as the Light of the world to guide humanity and lead it at last into the Promised Land where
freedom, justice, and peace reign. And we see more and
more clearly that on our own we cannot foster justice and
peace unless the light of a God who shows us his Face is
revealed to us, a God who appears to us in the manger of
Bethlehem, who appears to us on the Cross.

HOMILY, JANUARY 6, 2007

ENCOUNTERING THE RISEN CHRIST

In the light of the encounter with the Risen Christ, Paul
realized that as soon as they adhered to the Gospel of Jesus
Christ, the Gentiles no longer needed as a hallmark of
justice either circumcision or the rules that governed food
and the Sabbath: Christ is our justice and all things that
conform to him are "just."

GENERAL AUDIENCE, OCTOBER 1, 2008

COME, LORD JESUS!

The Church's evangelizing mission is the response to the
cry "Come, Lord Jesus" that pervades all of salvation history and continues to rise from believers' lips. Come,
Lord, transform our hearts, so that justice and peace may
be spread in the world!

ANGELUS, DECEMBER 23, 2007

Everything Meant to Serve Human Family

Certainly the building of a just society is the primary responsibility of the political order, both in individual States and in the international community. As such, it demands, at every level, a disciplined exercise of practical reason and a training of the will in order to discern and achieve the specific requirements of justice in full respect for the common good and the inalienable dignity of each individual. In my Encyclical *Deus Caritas Est*, I wished to reaffirm, at the beginning of my Pontificate, the Church's desire to contribute to this necessary purification of reason, to help form consciences and to stimulate a greater response to the genuine requirements of justice. At the same time, I wished to emphasize that, even in the most just society, there will always be a place for charity: "there is no ordering of the State so just that it can eliminate the need for a service of love" (No. 28).

The Church's conviction of the inseparability of justice and charity is ultimately born of her experience of the revelation of God's infinite justice and mercy in Jesus Christ, and it finds expression in her insistence that man himself and his irreducible dignity must be at the center of political and social life. Her teaching, which is addressed not only to believers but to all people of good will, thus appeals to right reason and a sound understanding of human nature in proposing principles capable of guiding individuals and communities in the pursuit of a social order marked by justice, freedom, fraternal solidarity, and peace.

At the heart of that teaching, as you well know, is the principle of the universal destination of all the goods of creation. According to this fundamental principle, everything that the earth produces and all that man transforms and manufactures, all his knowledge and technology, is meant to serve the material and spiritual development and fulfillment of the human family and all its members.

LETTER, APRIL 28, 2007

HARMONIOUS COEXISTENCE

Peace thus comes to be seen in a new light: not as the mere absence of war, but as a harmonious coexistence of individual citizens within a society governed by justice, one in which the good is also achieved, to the extent possible, for each of them. The truth of peace calls upon everyone to cultivate productive and sincere relationships; it encourages them to seek out and to follow the paths of forgiveness and reconciliation, to be transparent in their dealings with others, and to be faithful to their word. In a particular way, the followers of Christ, recognizing the insidious presence of evil and the need for that liberation brought by the divine Master, look to him with confidence, in the knowledge that "he committed no sin; no guile was found on his lips" (*1 Pet* 2:22; cf. *Is* 53:9). Jesus defined himself as the Truth in person, and, in addressing the seer of the Book of Revelation, he states his complete aversion to "every one who loves and practices falsehood" (*Rev* 22:15). He has disclosed the full truth about humanity and about human history. The power of his grace makes it possible to live "in" and "by" truth, since he alone is completely true and faithful. Jesus is the truth which gives us peace.

MESSAGE, JANUARY 1, 2006

CHAPTER 6

FORTITUDE

Fortitude ensures firmness in difficulties and constancy in the pursuit of the good. (*CCC* 1837)

■

On the day I called, thou didst answer me, my strength of soul thou didst increase. (*Ps* 138:3)

THE FLAME OF LOVE

However, in the coded language of the Seer of Patmos it contains a precise reference to the clear flame of love that impelled Christ to pour out his blood for us. By virtue of that blood, we have been purified. Sustained by that flame, the martyrs too poured out their blood and were purified in love: in the love of Christ who made them capable of sacrificing themselves for love in their turn. Jesus said: "Greater love has no man than this, that a man lay down his life for his friends" (*Jn* 15:13). Every witness of faith lives this "greater love" and, after the example of the Divine Teacher, is ready to sacrifice his life for the

Kingdom. In this way we become friends of Christ; thus, we are conformed to him, accepting the extreme sacrifice without limiting the gift of love and the service of faith.

HOMILY, APRIL 7, 2008

FORTITUDE AND WITNESS GIVE COURAGE

We will continue our journey towards World Youth Day 2008 by reflecting on the *Spirit of Fortitude and Witness* that gives us the courage to live according to the Gospel and to proclaim it boldly. Therefore it is very important that each one of you young people — in your communities, and together with those responsible for your education — should be able to reflect on this Principal Agent of salvation history, namely the Holy Spirit or the Spirit of Jesus. In this way you will be able to achieve the following lofty goals: to recognize the Spirit's true identity, principally by listening to the Word of God in the Revelation of the Bible; to become clearly aware of his continuous, active presence in the life of the Church, especially as you rediscover that the Holy Spirit is the "soul," the vital breath of Christian life itself, through the sacraments of Christian initiation — Baptism, Confirmation, and the Eucharist; to grow thereby in an understanding of Jesus that becomes ever deeper and more joyful and, at the same time, to put the Gospel into practice at the dawn of the third millennium. In this message I gladly offer you an outline for meditation that you can explore during this year of preparation. In this way you can test the quality of your faith in the Holy Spirit, rediscover it if it is lost, strengthen it if it has become weak, savor it as fellowship with the Father and with his Son Jesus Christ, brought about by the indispensable working of the Holy Spirit. Never forget that the Church, in fact humanity itself, all the people around you now and those who await you in the future, expect much from you young people, because you have within you the supreme gift of the Father, the Spirit of Jesus.

MESSAGE TO THE YOUNG PEOPLE OF THE WORLD, JULY 20, 2007

REMAINING FAITHFUL TO THE LORD

During the Old Testament, God revealed himself partially, gradually, as we all do in our personal relationships. It took time for the chosen people to develop their relationship with God. The Covenant with Israel was like a period of courtship, a long engagement. Then came the definitive moment, the moment of marriage, the establishment of a new and everlasting covenant. As Mary stood before the Lord, she represented the whole of humanity. In the angel's message, it was as if God made a marriage proposal to the human race. And in our name, Mary said yes.

In fairy tales, the story ends there, and all "live happily ever after." In real life it is not so simple. For Mary there were many struggles ahead, as she lived out the consequences of the "yes" that she had given to the Lord. Simeon prophesied that a sword would pierce her heart. When

Jesus was twelve years old, she experienced every parent's worst nightmare when, for three days, the child went missing. And after his public ministry, she suffered the agony of witnessing his crucifixion and death. Throughout her trials she remained faithful to her promise, sustained by the Spirit of fortitude. And she was gloriously rewarded.

Dear young people, we too must remain faithful to the "yes" that we have given to the Lord's offer of friendship. We know that he will never abandon us. We know that he will always sustain us through the gifts of the Spirit. Mary accepted the Lord's "proposal" in our name. So let us turn to her and ask her to guide us as we struggle to remain faithful to the life-giving relationship that God has established with each one of us. She is our example and our inspiration, she intercedes for us with her Son, and with a mother's love she shields us from harm.

ANGELUS, JULY 20, 2008

OVERCOMING TRIALS

I cordially greet ... all those who have come to celebrate the canonization of St. Alphonsa of the Immaculate Conception. Her heroic virtues of patience, fortitude, and perseverance in the midst of deep suffering remind us that God always provides the strength we need to overcome every trial.

ANGELUS, OCTOBER 12, 2008

Spiritual Vitality Needed

We are gathered this evening in a place that is dear to you, a place that is a visible sign of the power of divine grace acting in the hearts of believers. The beauty of this thousand-year-old church is indeed a living testimony to your people's rich history of faith and Christian tradition: a history that is illuminated in particular by the faithfulness of those who sealed their adherence to Christ and to the Church by martyrdom. I am thinking of Saint Wenceslaus, Saint Adalbert, and Saint John Nepomuk, milestones in your Church's history, to whom we may add the example of the young Saint Vitus, who preferred to die a martyr's death rather than betray Christ, and the examples of the monk Saint Procopius and Saint Ludmila. From the twentieth century, I recall the experiences of two Archbishops of this local Church, Cardinals Josef Beran and František Tomášek, and of many Bishops, priests, men and women religious, and lay faithful, who resisted Communist persecution with heroic fortitude, even to the sacrifice of their lives. Where did these courageous friends of Christ find their strength if not from the Gospel? Indeed, they were captivated by Jesus who said: "If any man would come after me, let him deny himself and take up his cross and follow me" (*Mt* 16:24). In the hour of trial they heard another saying of Jesus resounding deep within them: "If they persecuted me, they will persecute you" (*Jn* 15:20).

The heroism of these witnesses to the faith reminds us that only through personal intimacy and a profound bond with Christ is it possible to draw the spiritual vitality needed to live the Christian vocation to the full. Only the love of Christ can make the apostolate effective, especially in moments of difficulty and trial. Love for Christ and for one's fellow men and women must be the hallmark of every Christian and every community. In the *Acts of the Apostles* we read that "the company of those who believed were of one heart and soul" (4:32). Tertullian, an early Church writer, noted that pagans were impressed by the love that bound Christians together (cf. *Apologeticum* XXXIX). Dear brothers and sisters, imitate the divine Master who "came not to be served, but to serve, and to give his life as a ransom for many" (*Mk* 10:45). Let love shine forth in each of your parishes and communities, and in your various associations and movements. According to the image used by Saint Paul, let your Church be a well-structured body with Christ as Head, in which every member acts in harmony with the whole. Nourish your love for Christ by prayer and listening to his word; feed on him in the Eucharist, and by his grace, be builders of unity and peace wherever you go.

ADDRESS, SEPTEMBER 26, 2009 (VISIT TO CZECH REPUBLIC)

THE BREATH OF GOD

Lastly, a final thought may also be found in the account of the Acts of the Apostles: the Holy Spirit overcomes fear. We know that the disciples sought shelter in the Upper Room after the arrest of their Lord and that they had remained isolated for fear of suffering the same fate. After Jesus' Resurrection their fear was not suddenly dispelled. But here at Pentecost, when the Holy Spirit rested upon them, those men emerged fearless and began to proclaim the Good News of the Crucified and Risen Christ to all. They were not afraid because they felt they were in the hands of the strongest One. Yes, dear brothers and sisters, wherever the Spirit of God enters he puts fear to flight; he makes us know and feel that we are in the hands of an Omnipotence of love: something happens, his infinite love does not abandon us. It is demonstrated by the witness of martyrs, by the courage of confessors of the faith, by the undaunted zeal of missionaries, by the frankness of preachers, by the example of all the saints, even some who were adolescents and children. It is demonstrated by the very existence of the Church which, despite the limitations and sins of men and women, continues to cross the ocean of history, blown by the breath of God and enlivened by his purifying fire. With this faith and joyful hope let us repeat today, through the intercession of Mary: *"Send forth your Spirit, O Lord, and renew the face of the earth."*

HOMILY, MAY 31, 2009

THE JOY BORN OF TRUTH

The incarnate Word, Word of Truth, makes us free and directs our freedom towards the good. My dear young friends, meditate often on the word of God, and allow the Holy Spirit to be your teacher. You will then discover that

God's way of thinking is not the same as that of human-kind's. You will find yourselves led to contemplate the real God and to read the events of history through his eyes. You will savor in fullness the joy that is born of truth. On life's journey, which is neither easy nor free of deceptions, you will meet difficulties and suffering and at times you will be tempted to exclaim with the psalmist: "I am sorely afflicted" (*Ps* 119 [118], v. 107). Do not forget to add as the psalmist did: "give me life, O LORD, according to your word.... I hold my life in my hand continually, but I do not forget thy law" (*ibid.*, vv. 107; 109). The loving presence of God, through his word, is the lamp that dispels the darkness of fear and lights up the path even when times are most difficult.

MESSAGE, APRIL 9, 2006

LET THE HOLY SPIRIT DESCEND

Dear brothers and sisters, the first Pentecost took place when Mary Most Holy was present amid the disciples in the Upper Room in Jerusalem and prayed. Today, too, let us entrust ourselves to her maternal intercession, so that the Holy Spirit may descend in abundance upon the Church in our day, fill the hearts of all the faithful and enkindle in them the fire of his love.

REGINA CAELI, MAY 27, 2007

NEED FOR DISCIPLES OF CHRIST

Let us not forget that the greater the gift of God — and the gift of the Spirit of Jesus is the greatest of all — so much the greater is the world's need to receive it and therefore the greater and the more exciting is the Church's mission to bear credible witness to it. You young people, through World Youth Day, are in a way manifesting your desire to participate in this mission. In this regard, my dear young friends, I want to remind you here of some key truths on which to meditate. Once again I repeat that only Christ can fulfill the most intimate aspirations that are in the heart of each person. Only Christ can humanize humanity and lead it to its "divinization." Through the power of his Spirit he instills divine charity within us, and this makes us capable of loving our neighbor and ready to be of service. The Holy Spirit enlightens us, revealing Christ crucified and risen, and shows us how to become more like Him so that we can be "the image and instrument of the love which flows from Christ" (*Deus Caritas Est*, 33). Those who allow themselves to be led by the Spirit understand that placing oneself at the service of the Gospel is not an optional extra, because they are aware of the urgency of transmitting this Good News to others. Nevertheless, we need to be reminded again that we can be witnesses of Christ only if we allow ourselves to be led by the Holy Spirit who is "the principal agent of evangelization" (cf. *Evangelii Nuntiandi*, 75) and "the principal agent of mission" (cf. *Redemptoris Missio*, 21). My dear young friends, as my venerable predecessors Paul VI and John Paul II said on several occasions, to proclaim the Gospel and bear witness to the faith is more necessary than ever today (cf. *Redemptoris Missio*, 1). There are those who think that to present the precious treasure of faith to people who do not share it means being intolerant towards them, but this is not the case, because to present Christ is not to impose Him (cf. *Evangelii Nuntiandi*, 80). Moreover, two thousand years ago twelve Apostles gave their lives to make Christ known and loved. Throughout the centuries since then, the Gospel has continued to spread by means of men and women inspired by that same missionary fervor. Today too there is a need for disciples of Christ who give unstintingly of their time and energy to serve the Gospel. There is a need for young people who will allow God's love to burn within them and who will respond generously to his urgent call, just as many young blesseds and saints did in the past and also in more recent times. In particular, I assure you that the Spirit of Jesus today is inviting you young people to be bearers of the good news of Jesus to your contemporaries.

MESSAGE TO THE YOUNG PEOPLE OF THE WORLD, JULY 20, 2007

BE MY WITNESSES

The Holy Spirit, therefore, is the power through which Christ causes us to experience his closeness. But the first reading also has something else to say: you will be my witnesses. The Risen Christ needs witnesses who have met him, people who have known him intimately through the power of the Holy Spirit; those who have, so to speak, actually touched him, can witness to him.

It is in this way that the Church, the family of Christ, "beginning at Jerusalem"..., as the Reading says, spread to the very ends of the earth. It is through witnesses that the Church was built — starting with Peter and Paul and the Twelve, to the point of including all who, filled with Christ, have rekindled down the centuries and will rekindle the flame of faith in a way that is ever new. All Christians in their own way can and must be witnesses of the Risen Lord.

HOMILY, MAY 7, 2005

UNITY AND MISSION OF CHURCH

Of particular joy for our Churches has been the participation of the Ecumenical Patriarch of Constantinople, His Holiness Bartholomew I, at the recent Synod of Bishops in Rome dedicated to the theme: *The Word of God in the Life and Mission of the Church*. The warm welcome he received and his moving intervention were sincere expressions of the deep spiritual joy that arises from the extent to which communion is already present between our Churches. Such ecumenical experience bears clear witness to the link between the unity of the Church and her mission. Extending his arms on the Cross, Jesus revealed the fullness of his desire to draw all people to himself, uniting them together as one (cf. *Jn* 12:32). Breathing his Spirit upon us he revealed his power to enable us to participate in his mission of reconciliation (cf. *Jn* 19:30; 20:22–23). In that breath, through the redemption that unites, stands our mission! Little wonder, then, that it is precisely in our burning desire to bring Christ to others, to make known his message of reconciliation (cf. 2 *Cor* 5:19), that we experience the shame of our division. Yet, sent out into the world (cf. *Jn* 20:21), empowered by the unifying force of the Holy Spirit (*ibid.*, v. 22), proclaiming the reconciliation that draws all to believe that Jesus is the Son of God (*ibid.*, v. 31), we shall find the strength to redouble our efforts to perfect our communion, to make it complete, to bear united witness to the love of the Father who sends the Son so that the world may know his love for us (cf. *Jn* 17:23).

ADDRESS, MAY 15, 2009

MAKING A CONTRIBUTION

Christ's presence is a gift that we must be able to share with everyone. It is for this purpose that the diocesan community is making an effort to form pastoral workers, so as to equip them to respond to the challenges modern culture poses to the Christian faith. The presence of numerous highly qualified academic institutions in Rome and the many initiatives promoted by the parishes enable us to look confidently to the future of Christianity in this city. As you well know, encountering Christ renews our personal life and helps us to contribute to building a just and fraternal society. This is why we as believers can also make a great contribution to overcoming the current educational emergency. Thus, for a profound evangelization and a courageous human promotion that can communicate the riches that derive from the encounter with Christ to as many people as possible, an increase in synergy among families, school, and parishes is more important than ever. For this I encourage each member of our diocese to continue on the journey they have undertaken, together carrying out the program for the current pastoral year which aims precisely to "educate to hope through prayer, action, and suffering."

HOMILY, DECEMBER 31, 2008

HUMILITY IS REQUIRED

The "Repent and believe in the Gospel" is not only at the beginning of Christian life but accompanies it throughout, endures, is renewed, and spreads, branching out into all its expressions. Every day is a favorable moment of grace because every day presses us to give ourselves to Jesus, to trust in him, to abide in him, to share his lifestyle, to learn true love from him, to follow him in the daily fulfillment of the Father's will, the one great law of life. Every day, even when it is fraught with difficulties and toil, weariness and setbacks, even when we are tempted to leave the path of the following of Christ and withdraw into ourselves, into our selfishness, without realizing our need to open ourselves to the love of God in Christ, to live the same logic of justice and love. In my recent Message for Lent I wanted to recall that "humility is required to accept that I need Another to free me from "what is mine," to give me gratuitously "what is His." This happens especially in the sacraments of Reconciliation and the Eucharist. Thanks to Christ's action, we may enter into the "greatest" justice, which is that of love (cf. *Rom* 13:8–10), the justice that recognizes itself in every case more a debtor than a creditor, because it has received more than could ever have been expected" (*Message*, 30 October 2009).

GENERAL AUDIENCE, FEBRUARY 10, 2010

SIGNS OF THE COVENANT

Indeed, the Psalmist confesses that he will "adore before your holy temple" in Jerusalem (cf. *Ps* 138, [137], v. 2): there he sings before God, who is in heaven with his court of angels but is also listening in the earthly space of the temple (cf. v. 1). The person praying is sure that the "name" of the Lord, that is, his personal reality, alive and active, and his virtues of faithfulness and mercy, signs of the Covenant with his people, are the support of all faithfulness and hope (cf. *ibid.*, v. 2).

He then briefly turns his gaze to the past, to the day of affliction: at that time the divine voice answered the anguished cry of the believer. Indeed, it instilled courage in the distressed soul (cf. *ibid.*, v. 3). The original Hebrew speaks literally of the Lord who "increased the strength of soul" of the righteous one who is oppressed. It is as if an impetuous wind had broken into it, sweeping away hesitations and fears, instilling in it new, vital energy and making fortitude and faithfulness flourish.

General Audience, December 7, 2005

Fidelity to God

Fidelity to God is a gift of his grace. Therefore, St. Hilary asks, at the end of his *Treatise on the Trinity*, to be able to remain ever faithful to the baptismal faith. It is a feature of this book: reflection is transformed into prayer and prayer returns to reflection. The whole book is a dialogue with God.

I would like to end today's Catechesis with one of these prayers, which thus becomes our prayer:

"Obtain, O Lord," St. Hilary recites with inspiration, "that I may keep ever faithful to what I have professed in the symbol of my regeneration, when I was baptized in the Father, in the Son, and in the Holy Spirit. That I may worship you, our Father, and with you, your Son; that I may deserve your Holy Spirit, who proceeds from you through your Only Begotten Son.... Amen" (*De Trinitate* 12, 57).

General Audience, October 10, 2007

Being Attentive to God's Word

From this moment onwards, my dear young friends, in a climate of constant listening to the word of God, call on the Holy Spirit, *Spirit of fortitude and witness*, that you may be able to proclaim the Gospel without fear even to the ends of the earth. Our Lady was present in the cenacle with the Apostles as they waited for Pentecost. May she be your mother and guide. May she teach you to receive the word of God, to treasure it and to ponder on it in your heart (cf *Lk* 2:19) as she did throughout her life. May she encourage you to declare your "yes" to the Lord as you live "the obedience of faith." May she help you to remain strong in the faith, constant in hope, persevering in charity, always attentive to the word of God. I am together with you in prayer, and I bless each one of you with all my heart.

MESSAGE, APRIL 9, 2006

CHAPTER 7

TEMPERANCE

**Temperance moderates the attraction of
the pleasures of the senses and provides
balance in the use of created goods.
(*CCC* 1838)**

■

**Wine is like life to men, if you drink it
in moderation. What is life to a man
who is without wine? It has been created
to make men glad. (*Sir* 31:27)**

CONTRIBUTING TO THE COMMON GOOD

The religious sense planted within the human heart opens
men and women to God and leads them to discover that
personal fulfillment does not consist in the selfish gratification of ephemeral desires. Rather, it leads us to meet
the needs of others and to search for concrete ways to
contribute to the common good. Religions have a special
role in this regard, for they teach people that authentic
service requires sacrifice and self-discipline, which in turn
must be cultivated through self-denial, temperance, and a

moderate use of the world's goods. In this way, men and women are led to regard the environment as a marvel to be pondered and respected rather than a commodity for mere consumption. It is incumbent upon religious people to demonstrate that it is possible to find joy in living simply and modestly, generously sharing one's surplus with those suffering from want.

ADDRESS, JULY 18, 2008

SAVIOR FOR TODAY

[D]oes a "Savior" still have any value and meaning *for the men and women of the third millennium*? Is a "Savior" still needed by a humanity which has reached the moon and Mars and is prepared to conquer the universe; for a humanity which knows no limits in its pursuit of nature's secrets and which has succeeded even in deciphering the marvelous codes of the human genome? Is a Savior needed by a humanity which has invented interactive communication, which navigates in the virtual ocean of the internet and, thanks to the most advanced modern communications technologies, has now made the Earth, our great common home, a global village? This humanity of the twenty-first century appears as a sure and self-sufficient master of its own destiny, the avid proponent of uncontested triumphs.

… "*Salvator noster*": Christ is also the Savior of men and women today. Who will make this message of hope resound, in a credible way, in every corner of the earth? Who will work to ensure the recognition, protection, and promotion of the integral good of the human person as the condition for peace, respecting each man and every woman and their proper dignity? Who will help us to realize that with good will, reasonableness, and moderation it is possible to avoid aggravating conflicts and instead to find fair solutions?

Urbi et Orbi Message, Christmas, 2006

Choosing Poverty

Thus it is necessary to seek to establish a "virtuous circle" between the poverty "to be chosen" and the poverty "to be fought." This gives access to a path rich in fruits for humanity's present and future and which could be summarized thus: to fight the evil poverty that oppresses so many men and women and threatens the peace of all, it is necessary to rediscover moderation and solidarity as evangelical, and at the same time universal, values. More practically, it is impossible to combat poverty effectively unless one does what St. Paul wrote to the Corinthians, in other words if one does not seek "to create equality," reducing the gap between those who waste the superfluous and those who lack what they need. This entails just and sober decisions, which are moreover made obligatory by the need to administer the earth's limited resources wisely. When he says that Jesus Christ "for [our] sake became poor," St. Paul offers an important indication not only from the theological point of view but also at the sociological level; not in the sense that poverty is a value in itself, but because it is a condition that demonstrates solidarity. When Francis of Assisi stripped himself of his possessions, it was a decision to witness that was inspired in him directly by God, but at the same time it shows everyone the way of trust in Providence. Thus, in the Church, the vow of poverty is the commitment of some, but it reminds all of the need to be detached from material goods and of the primacy of spiritual riches. This is therefore the message for us today: the poverty of Christ's Birth in Bethlehem, as well as being the subject of adoration for Christians, is also a school of life for every man. It teaches us that to fight both material and spiritual poverty, the path to take is the path of solidarity that impelled Jesus to share our human condition.

HOMILY, JANUARY 1, 2009

ASPIRE TO LIVE GENEROUSLY

One of the many ways religion stands at the service of mankind is by offering a vision of the human person that highlights our innate aspiration to live generously, forging bonds of friendship with our neighbors. At their core, human relations cannot be defined in terms of power, domination, and self-interest. Rather, they reflect and perfect man's natural inclination to live in communion and accord with others.

The religious sense planted within the human heart opens men and women to God and leads them to discover that personal fulfillment does not consist in the selfish gratification of ephemeral desires. Rather, it leads us to meet the needs of others and to search for concrete ways to contribute to the common good. Religions have a special role in this regard, for they teach people that authentic service requires sacrifice and self-discipline, which in turn must be cultivated through self-denial, temperance, and a moderate use of the world's goods. In this way, men and women are led to regard the environment as a marvel to be pondered and respected rather than a commodity for mere consumption. It is incumbent upon religious people to demonstrate that it is possible to find joy in living simply and modestly, generously sharing one's surplus with those suffering from want.

ADDRESS, JULY 18, 2008

ADVENT'S COMMERCIAL POLLUTION

After celebrating the Solemnity of the Immaculate Conception of Mary, we enter during these days into the evocative atmosphere of immediate preparation for Holy Christmas, and we already see the tree set up here. In today's consumer society, this period has unfortunately suffered a sort of commercial "pollution" that risks changing its authentic spirit, marked by recollection, moderation, and joy, which is not external but intimate.

DECEMBER 11, 2005

A Monk's Journey

He [John Climacus] became famous, as I have already said, through his work, entitled *The Climax*, in the West known as the *Ladder of Divine Ascent* (*PG* 88, 632–1164). Composed at the insistent request of the hegumen of the neighboring Monastery of Raithu in Sinai, the *Ladder* is a complete treatise of spiritual life in which John describes the monk's journey from renunciation of the world to the perfection of love. This journey according to his book covers thirty steps, each one of which is linked to the next. The journey may be summarized in three consecutive stages: the first is expressed in renunciation of the world in order to return to a state of evangelical childhood. Thus, the essential is not the renunciation but rather the connection with what Jesus said, that is, the return to true childhood in the spiritual sense, becoming like children. John comments: "A good foundation of three layers and three pillars is: innocence, fasting, and temperance. Let all babes in Christ (cf. 1 *Cor* 3:1) begin with these virtues, taking as their model the natural babes" (1, 20; 636). Voluntary detachment from beloved people and places permits the soul to enter into deeper communion with God. This renunciation leads to obedience which is the way to humility through humiliations which will never be absent on the part of the brethren. John comments: "Blessed is he who has mortified his will to the very end and has entrusted the care of himself to his teacher in the Lord: indeed he will be placed on the right hand of the Crucified One!" (4, 37; 704).

GENERAL AUDIENCE, FEBRUARY 11, 2009

The Family as Church in Miniature

John Chrysostom was anxious to accompany his writings with the person's integral development in his physical, intellectual, and religious dimensions. The various phases of his growth are compared to as many seas in an immense ocean: "The first of these seas is childhood" (*Homily*, 81, 5 *on Matthew's Gospel*).

Indeed, "it is precisely at this early age that inclinations to vice or virtue are manifest." Thus, God's law must be impressed upon the soul from the outset "as on a wax tablet" (*Homily* 3, 1 *on John's Gospel*): This is indeed the most important age. We must bear in mind how fundamentally important it is that the great orientations which give man a proper outlook on life truly enter him in this first phase of life.

Chrysostom therefore recommended: "From the tenderest age, arm children with spiritual weapons and teach them to make the Sign of the Cross on their forehead with their hand" (*Homily*, 12, 7 *on First Corinthians*).

Then come adolescence and youth: "Following childhood is the sea of adolescence, where violent winds blow..., for concupiscence ... grows within us" (*Homily* 81, 5 *on Matthew's Gospel*).

Lastly comes engagement and marriage: "Youth is succeeded by the age of the mature person who assumes family commitments: this is the time to seek a wife" (*ibid.*).

He recalls the aims of marriage, enriching them — referring to virtue and temperance — with a rich fabric of personal relationships. Properly prepared spouses therefore bar the way to divorce: everything takes place with joy, and children can be educated in virtue. Then when the first child is born, he is "like a bridge; the three become one flesh, because the child joins the two parts" (*Homily* 12, 5 on the Letter to the Colossians), and the three constitute "a family, a Church in miniature" (*Homily* 20, 6 *on the Letter to the Ephesians*).

GENERAL AUDIENCE, SEPTEMBER 19, 2007

SERVANT LEADER

The ministerial priesthood entails a profound relationship with Christ who is given to us in the Eucharist. Let the celebration of the Eucharist be truly the center of your priestly lives; in this way it will also be the center of your ecclesial mission. Throughout our lives Christ calls us to share in his mission, to be his witnesses, so that his word may be proclaimed to all. In celebrating this sacrament in the Lord's name and in his person, the person of the priest cannot occupy center stage; he is a servant, a humble instrument pointing to Christ, who offers himself in sacrifice for the salvation of the world. As Jesus teaches us, the leader must become "as one who serves" (*Lk* 22:26). Origen writes that "Joseph understood that Jesus was superior to him even as he submitted to him, and, knowing the superiority of his charge, he commanded him with respect and moderation. Everyone should reflect on this: frequently a lesser man is placed over people who are greater, and it happens at times that an inferior is more worthy than the one who appears to be set above him. If a person of greater dignity understands this, then he will not be puffed up with pride because of his higher rank; he will know that his inferior may well be superior to him, even as Jesus was subject to Joseph" (*Homily on Saint Luke* XX, 5; S.C. p. 287).

ADDRESS, MARCH 18, 2009

IDOLS OF CONSUMER SOCIETY

What can be said of the fact that, in the current consumers' society, profit and success have become the new idols before which so many prostrate themselves? The consequence is that it has brought us to give value solely to who, as is often said, "is lucky" and has "fame," certainly not those who must laboriously battle with life each day. Possession of material goods and applause of the masses have replaced the work on oneself that serves to temper the spirit and form an authentic personality. One risks being superficial, taking dangerous short-cuts in the search for success, thus consigning life to experiences that give immediate satisfaction, but are in themselves precarious and misleading. The tendency toward individualism is growing, and when one is concentrated only on oneself, one inevitably becomes fragile; the capacity to listen is weakened, which is an indispensable stage in understanding others and working together.

ADDRESS, SEPTEMBER 7, 2008

UNIVERSAL CHURCH

The Church is Catholic: a community embracing peoples of all races and languages, and not limited to any one culture or particular social, economic or political system (cf. *Gaudium et Spes*, 42). She is at the service of the entire human family, freely sharing her gifts for the well-being of all. This gives her a connatural ability to foster unity and peace. My dear brothers, you and your people, as promoters of harmony and peace, have much to offer the nation. In your love for your country you inspire tolerance, moderation, and understanding. By encouraging people who share important values to cooperate for the common good, you help to consolidate your country's stability and to maintain it for the future. These efforts, however subtle, give effective support to the majority of your fellow citizens who uphold the country's noble tradition of mutual respect, tolerance, and social harmony. May you likewise continue to sustain and counsel Catholic lay people and all who wish to offer their service for the good of society in public office, social communications, in education, healthcare, and social assistance. May they always rejoice in the knowledge that Christ accepts as a gesture of personal love whatever good is done to the least of his brothers (cf. *Mt* 25:40).

ADDRESS TO THE BISHOPS OF BANGLADESH, JUNE 12, 2008

TREATING DISSENTERS KINDLY

For the twelve years of his ministry as a priest in the Antiochean Church, John [Chrysostom] deeply distinguished himself by his eminent skill at interpreting the Sacred Scriptures in a way that the faithful could understand. In his preaching, he strove zealously to strengthen the unity of the Church, reinvigorating the Christian identity in his listeners at a time in history when the Church was threatened both from within and without. He rightly intuited that Christian unity depends above all on a true understanding of the central mysteries of the Church's faith: the Most Blessed Trinity and the Incarnation of the Divine Word. Well aware, however, of the difficulties of these mysteries, John spared no effort in making the Church's Magisterium accessible to the simple people in her assembly, both in Antioch and later also in Constantinople (cf. Johannes Chrysostomus, *De Incomprehensibili dei Natura*, [SCh 28ff., 93-322]. Cf. id., *In illud: Pater meus usque modo operatur* [PG 63, 511-516]; id., *In illud: Filius ex se nihil facit* [PG 56, 247-256]). Nor did he omit to also address the dissenters, preferring to treat them with patience rather than coercion since he believed that in order to correct a theological error, "nothing is more effective than moderation and kindliness" (cf. Johannes Chrysostomus, *De Incomprehensibili dei Natura* 1, 352-353 [SCh 28ff., 132]).

LETTER, AUGUST 10, 2007

MODERATION AND FORGIVENESS

How often relations between individuals, between groups, and between peoples are marked not by love but

by selfishness, injustice, hatred, and violence! These are
the scourges of humanity, open and festering in every
corner of the planet, although they are often ignored and
sometimes deliberately concealed; wounds that torture the
souls and bodies of countless of our brothers and sisters.
They are waiting to be tended and healed by the glorious
wounds of our Risen Lord (cf. *1 Pet* 2:24–25) and by the
solidarity of people who, following in his footsteps, perform deeds of charity in his name, make an active commitment to justice, and spread luminous signs of hope in
areas bloodied by conflict and wherever the dignity of the
human person continues to be scorned and trampled. It is
hoped that these are precisely the places where gestures of
moderation and forgiveness will increase!

Dear brothers and sisters! Let us allow the light that
streams forth from this solemn day to enlighten us; let us
open ourselves in sincere trust to the risen Christ, so that
his victory over evil and death may also triumph in each
one of us, in our families, in our cities, and in our nations.
Let it shine forth in every part of the world.

URBI ET ORBI MESSAGE, EASTER 2008

GOD'S PASSIONATE LOVE FOR HIS PEOPLE

We have seen that God's *eros* for man is also totally *agape*.
This is not only because it is bestowed in a completely
gratuitous manner, without any previous merit, but also
because it is love which forgives. Hosea above all shows us
that this *agape* dimension of God's love for man goes far

beyond the aspect of gratuity. Israel has committed "adultery" and has broken the covenant; God should judge and repudiate her. It is precisely at this point that God is revealed to be God and not man: "How can I give you up, O Ephraim! How can I hand you over, O Israel!... My heart recoils within me, my compassion grows warm and tender. I will not execute my fierce anger, I will not again destroy Ephraim; for I am God and not man, the Holy One in your midst" (*Hos* 11:8–9). God's passionate love for his people — for humanity — is at the same time a forgiving love. It is so great that it turns God against himself, his love against his justice. Here Christians can see a dim prefigurement of the mystery of the Cross: so great is God's love for man that by becoming man he follows him even into death, and so reconciles justice and love.

ENCYCLICAL, *DEUS CARITAS EST*, No. 10

VOCATION OF BAPTISM

But how can the baptismal vocation be brought to fulfillment so as to be victorious in the struggle between the flesh and the spirit, between good and evil, a combat that marks our existence? In the Gospel passage today the Lord indicates to us three useful means: prayer, almsgiving, and fasting. We also find useful references to this in St. Paul's experience and writings. Concerning *prayer* he urges us to be "constant," and to be "watchful in it with thanksgiving" (*Rom* 12:12; *Col* 4:2), to "pray constantly" (*1 Thess* 5:17). Jesus is in the depths of our hearts. He makes himself present and his presence will remain, even if we speak and act in accordance with our professional duties. For this reason, in prayer there is within our hearts an inner presence of relationship with God, which gradually becomes also an explicit prayer. With regard to *almsgiving* the passages on the great collection for the poor brethren are certainly important (cf. *2 Cor* 8 and 9) but it should be noted that for St. Paul, love is the apex of the believer's life, "the bond of perfection"; "and above all these," he writes to the Colossians, "put on love, which binds everything together in perfect harmony" (*Col* 3:14). He does not speak specifically of *fasting* but urges people frequently to have moderation, as a characteristic of those who are called to live in watchful expectation of the Lord (cf. *1 Thess* 5:6–8; *Tit* 2:12). His reference to that spiritual "competitiveness" which calls for sobriety is also interesting: "Every athlete," he writes to the Corinthians, "exercises self-control in all things. They do it to receive a perishable wreath, but we an imperishable" (*1 Cor* 9:25). The Christian must be disciplined in order to discover the way and truly reach the Lord.

HOMILY, FEBRUARY 25, 2009

Freedom from Material Possessions

In addressing his monks, Theodore spoke in a practical, at times picturesque manner about poverty, but poverty in the following of Christ is from the start an essential element of monasticism and also points out a way for all of us. The renunciation of private property, this freedom from material things, as well as moderation and simplicity apply in a radical form only to monks, but the spirit of this renouncement is equal for all. Indeed, we must not depend on material possessions but instead must learn renunciation, simplicity, austerity, and moderation. Only in this way can a supportive society develop and the great problem of poverty in this world be overcome. Therefore, in this regard the monks' radical poverty is essentially also a path for us all. Then when he explains the temptations against chastity, Theodore does not conceal his own experience and indicates the way of inner combat to find self control and hence respect for one's own body and for the body of the other as a temple of God.

GENERAL AUDIENCE, MAY 27, 2009

Prayers

Act of Faith

O my God, I firmly believe that you are
one God in three divine Persons, Father,
Son, and Holy Spirit; I believe that your
divine Son became man and died for
our sins, and that he shall come to judge
the living and the dead. I believe these
and all the truths that the holy Catholic
Church teaches, because you have
revealed them, who can neither deceive
nor be deceived.

Act of Hope

O my God, relying on your almighty
power and infinite mercy and promises,
I hope to obtain pardon for my sins, the
help of your grace, and life everlasting,
through the merits of Jesus Christ, my
Lord and Redeemer.

ACT OF CHARITY (LOVE)

O my God, I love you above all things
with my whole heart and soul, because
you are all-good and worthy of all love.
I love my neighbor as myself for love
of you. I forgive all who have injured
me, and I ask pardon of all whom I
have injured.

Books by Pope Benedict XVI
from Our Sunday Visitor

The Apostles
Hardback and Paperback

The Fathers, Volume I
St. Clement to St. Augustine

The Fathers, Volume II
St. Leo to St. Bernard

The Apostles, Illustrated

The Fathers, Illustrated
Volume I – St. Clement to St. Paulinus of Nola
Volume II – St. Augustine to St. Maximus the Confessor

Breakfast with Benedict

Questions and Answers

Saint Paul the Apostle

Our Sunday Visitor Publishing
1-800-348-2440 ◆ www.osv.com